Rules for the Spiritual Life

Fr. José Guadalupe Treviño

RULES
for the
SPIRITUAL
LIFE

Translated by
Rev. Benjamin B. Hunt, C.S.P.

SOPHIA INSTITUTE PRESS
Manchester, New Hampshire

Sophia Institute Press
Box 5284, Manchester, NH 03108
1-800-888-9344
www.SophiaInstitute.com

Sophia Institute Press is a registered trademark of Sophia Institute.

paperback ISBN 978-1-64413-902-8

ebook ISBN ISBN 978-1-64413-903-5

Library of Congress Control Number: 2023938521

First printing

Contents

Rules for the Spiritual Life

Translator's Foreword

In *Rules for the Spiritual Life*, Fr. J. G. Treviño, one of the most prolific of contemporary spiritual writers, presents a sort of ground plan for spiritual activity. Beginning with the importance of avoiding even semideliberate venial sin, he conducts the soul to the brink of the transforming union, there to have a glimpse of "hidden things which it is not given to a man to utter." Along the way he carefully points out and skirts the pitfalls, guiding the traveler securely along the path of Christian perfection.

Fr. Trevino originally titled his work *Rules of Spiritual Direction*, not that he meant the book as a guide to spiritual directors—although it might serve somewhat in that capacity—nor that he intended it as an adequate substitute for a spiritual director. But the work does, however, supply for a director in the broad sense that it combines theoretical principles and practical directives as a spiritual director might, in order to take the soul along the spiritual way. The book is at once doctrinal and very concretely practical.

The eighteen rules are the equivalent of eighteen chapters. Total surrender of the soul to God is the key to the whole book. The earlier rules are meant to prepare the way for total surrender, the later rules to carry it through. The first thing necessary for total surrender is the determination to get rid of all deliberate sin and affection for sin (Rule 1). This requires the perfect supernaturalization of the motives out of which we act (Rule 2). To grow in virtue, we must learn to accept and to love humiliations (Rule 4); mortification must become our daily food (Rule 6), adversity our consolation (Rule 7).

But it is essential that in our newfound dedication to spiritual things we avoid exaggerations and extremes (Rule 3). Holiness is to be found essentially in the constant and faithful fulfillment of our daily duty (Rule 9), and like Rome it cannot be built up all in one day (Rule 5). What we give up in the spiritual life we give up because of love (Rule 4). In fact, as the eye of the maidservant is on her mistress so is our eye to be on Jesus our divine Model (Rule 8). Union with Him must be our total desire (Rules 10, 13).

In keeping our view on our lofty goal, we must be mindful of the danger of falling from our first fervor (Rule 11) and reflect on the truth that to *live* the spiritual life is to grow in it (Rule 12). When at last we totally make ourselves over to God (Rule 14), we must not permit our offering to be vague and abstract; we must make it practical and concrete (Rule 15). Surrendered to God, we are to live in a peace that the world cannot give (Rule 16), always aware that it is the interior that gives our religious life its soul and its substance (Rule 17). The loftiness of the experiences of God's great mystics is at least a reminder of the sublimity of our Christian vocation (Rule 18), the end of which is that God may be all in all (Conclusion).

—The Translator

Rule 1

We must begin by tearing out at the roots affection for even semideliberate venial sin. In order to do this, we must value purity of soul passionately, above everything else, at the same time avoiding scrupulosity.

A man trying to make his way along a road blocked with obstacles must first get rid of the obstacles. On the road to perfection, the first and greatest obstacle is sin. Let us suppose mortal sin has been removed by a sincere conversion to God. The obstacle of venial sin remains, and in striving to get rid of it, we must be guided by sound principles.

First, we must keep in mind that the greatest trouble does not come from the venial sins into which we fall occasionally and through frailty. Because of our great weakness and misery, we cannot except by a special grace of God be completely free from falls of this sort.

Second, we must remember that the great obstacle on the road to perfection is affection for sin. Sins that arise from affection for sin generally proceed not from weakness or ignorance but from malice. They are not usually isolated acts but spring from genuine habits. If we entertain affection for venial sin in general, we are in the unfortunate state of lukewarmness. If the affection is for only a particular kind of sin, then there is still present a defect that the will is not disposed to correct and that places an obstacle to progress in grace. Individuals who entertain affection for sin remain bogged down on the road to perfection.

St. Thomas Aquinas says that "the chief duty of beginners is to avoid sin." Our first rule simply makes this more concrete by affirming that "it is necessary to tear out by the roots affection for venial sins, even semideliberate ones."

There are four steps in this task. (1) We have to eliminate venial sin. (2) We have to get rid of affection for sin. (3) We must tear out this affection by its roots. (4) We must work to free ourselves not only of deliberate but also of semideliberate venial sin. The most perfect way of avoiding venial sin is to get rid of every affection for it; the most efficacious way of getting rid of the affection is to tear it out radically; and the whole goal is best attained by combating not only deliberate but also semideliberate venial sin.

Now, how are we to tear out this affection by its roots? The root or cause of an affection is generally the dominant fault, or the inordinate attachment to something created. To root out affection for venial sin, we must discover and combat this dominant failing. Or better, we must attack the disordered attachment that gives rise to affection for sin. But there is a more general means of fighting affection for venial sin. In order to win this battle, we have to fight the enemy with his own weapons. We must fight affection with affection. And so the most universal and, at the same time, the most efficacious means for rooting out affection for venial sin is the love of purity of soul—a love so alive, so intense, so efficacious and ardent that it can justifiably be called a passion.

By analogy with the sensible passions, we give the name of *passion* to two supernatural affections that are generally found in those who serve God wholeheartedly: *the love of purity* and *the love of sacrifice*. Passionate love of purity and sacrifice is the fruit of the gifts of fear, knowledge, understanding, and wisdom. If we beg the Holy Spirit to set our soul aflame with these divine passions, and if we are faithful to the illuminations and motions that come from Him, we will succeed in acquiring the perfect purity of soul demanded by this rule.

In working to get rid of sin, we must take equal care to avoid scruples, or vain fear of sin where there is no sin. If an act is lawful or if advertence and consent are lacking, there is no sin. Delicacy of conscience must not be confused with scrupulosity. Scrupulosity causes distress; delicacy of conscience does not. Scrupulosity is born of a groundless fear, while delicacy of conscience proceeds from a holy fear of God, from that filial fear that makes one avoid everything that could be displeasing to one's heavenly Father. A delicate conscience will distinguish with unfailing care between mortal sin and venial, between venial sin and imperfection, between what God commands and what He counsels.

The first step, then, on the path to perfection is self-purification. And here lies not only the beginning but also the end, the golden thread that binds all the stages of the spiritual life together.

Rule 2

If we desire to progress in virtue, we must purify our heart and supernaturalize our affections.

We have just seen that the first step in the spiritual life consists in the removal of the first and greatest obstacle to perfection: sin. This is the same as saying that the soul must be purified. The second rule also speaks of purity, of the purification of the heart and the affections.

One sometimes hears the assertion that virtue dries up the heart. A widespread prejudice affirms that one cannot arrive at holiness without inhumanly disemboweling himself of all affections, even the most lawful. The severe words of our Lord are alleged: "If anyone comes to me and does not hate his father and mother ... he cannot be my disciple" (Luke 14:26).

Now such an opinion is absolutely erroneous. The essence of holiness lies in love or charity. Christian charity is essentially universal, extending to all men, whether relatives or foreigners, acquaintances or strangers, friends or enemies. Charity can exclude no one. In fact, by positively excluding from his charity any human being whatsoever, a person would sin against charity.

Charity does two things. First, it puts legitimate affections in proper order. As the spouse says in the Canticle of Canticles: "He set in order charity in me" (2:4). Second, it suppresses affections incompatible with the love of God.

Among affections we can distinguish lawful and unlawful. And within the lawful we find ordinate and inordinate. Every affection that cannot be indulged without offense to God is unlawful or sinful. For example, a married man cannot lawfully have conjugal affection toward any person except his wife. Toward any other person this affection is unlawful. Someone consecrated to God in the religious state cannot lawfully entertain this affection toward any person whatsoever. Unlawful also are all affections that are the proximate or remote occasion of sin. Now it is easy to understand why charity must suppress all these unlawful affections. If they are gravely sinful, they are completely incompatible with charity; if they are lightly sinful, they are an obstacle to the development and growth of charity.

All affections are lawful that do not of themselves imply offense to God. But even these will be inordinate when not subordinated to the love of God or when not supernaturalized. To understand this properly, we must distinguish natural from supernatural affections. In reality, there is no other supernatural love or affection besides charity, a single virtue through which we love God, and our neighbor because of God.

Natural affections are those that correspond to human nature, without reference to elevation to the supernatural order. In man there are two powers for loving, one sensible and the other spiritual. From this there result two classes of affections, sensible and spiritual—*spiritual* being here understood not in the sense of supernatural but simply as opposed to material. An example of a sensible affection is that which a man has for his dog or his horse, or for some human being purely because of physical beauty. Examples of spiritual or immaterial affection are those that the scientist has for knowledge, the philosopher for wisdom, the hero for his country, the upright man for duty, the gentleman for honor.

The work of charity with respect to these lawful affections is to order them. In what does this order consist? First, it consists in moderating the affections. All sensible affections, by the very fact that they belong to the sphere of the passions, tend to excess; and what they lack in consistency they make up for in impetuosity. They must be kept within the limits indicated by reason illuminated by faith.

Ordinarily, the practical way of moderating a sensible affection is to suppress, or at least diminish, its sensible manifestations. The reason for this is that in a sensible affection everything is sensible: the sense faculty or appetite that produces it, its object, and the external expressions that manifest it. Take, for example, a friendship that is purely sensible. The faculty that produces it is what the theologians call concupiscible appetite. Its object consists in the sensible qualities of one's friend. It manifests itself in affectionate actions and words. Practically speaking, to moderate this affection is to moderate its manifestations, even supposing, as we are supposing in fact, that they are lawful manifestations. Consequently, we ought not to converse with this friend purely for the pleasure of conversing but only when there is a reasonable motive; and even having a reasonable motive, we should not waste time in excessively long conversations. Likewise, we ought not to do favors that are unreasonable, favors that are not proportionate to our own resources and justified by a reasonable motive such as gratitude or helpfulness.

In the second place, charity orders our lawful affections by subordinating them to the love of God. Charity would not be charity if by it we did not love God above all else. Therefore, our Lord says: "He who loves father or mother more than me is not worthy of me" (Matt. 10:37). When the love of our parents comes into conflict with the love of God, we must prefer the love of God, as many a young man and woman have done in answering God's call to the religious life. To embrace the religious life is to separate oneself from one's parents, and this sometimes occasions great pain.

To subordinate natural affections to the love of God consists, then, in putting natural affections in the second place with reference to the love of God, and in being disposed to give them up entirely when they are in conflict with this same divine love.

In the third place, charity orders our natural affections by supernaturalizing them or making them "divine." It is a principle of capital importance in Christianity that everything must be supernatural. The spiritual life cannot be relegated to certain hours nor to a certain part of a person's being, even the higher part. The Christian must be wholly supernaturalized, in body and soul, in the faculties of the soul and the senses of the body, in his association with God and his association with creatures, in his intellectual, sensitive, and vegetative life, in his social and political relations. In a word, the whole man must be supernaturalized. Holiness and perfection are in reality nothing but the perfect divinization of the Christian. This divinization results when the Holy Spirit, by means of grace, the virtues, and the gifts, and especially charity, invades the whole of our being and the whole of our activity. It is the prelude to the perfect glorification of eternity, where all our being will, in a certain way, lose itself in God as a drop of water in the ocean.

Nothing is really so easy of accomplishment as a supernatural act. In order that an act of a just man be supernatural, two conditions suffice: first, the state of grace; second, that the act itself have a reasonable end. An act is more perfectly supernaturalized when a person has an actual or at least virtual intention of doing it for God.

The importance of this second rule lies in this, that God will never fill any soul until that soul is fully purified of all affections incompatible with charity, and until all lawful affections have been set in perfect order. Charity puts the natural affections of the soul in order by moderating them, by subordinating them to the love of God, and by supernaturalizing them.

Rule 3

In the work of sanctification, we must above all avoid exaggerations and extremes and strive for perfect balance.

A reed shaken by the slightest breeze, a leaf snatched up in a whirlwind, a cloud forever changing shape—such are the images with which Sacred Scripture represents the life of man—troubled, agitated, changing. Man is endowed with reason to lead him along the straight road of virtue. Yet he is often the plaything of his passions. He passes his days oscillating from extreme to extreme, unable to maintain that famous golden mean that is the object of the moral virtues.

A person leading a life of sin frequently has a conscience so lax as almost not to notice wrongdoing. When by the grace of God and a change of disposition he begins to lead a life of fervor, he often tightens and trims his conscience quite unnaturally and goes to a new extreme, that of scrupulosity. Now a scrupulous person who does not work to cure himself of his malady may so burden himself as to make virtue seemingly insupportable. God's convert goes back to his old ways, and the last state is worse than the first. A sound conscience is a balanced one.

Consider a person dominated by pride. If those who undertake to correct him repeat constantly that he is worth nothing, he may finally believe that statement quite literally. Thinking himself incapable of anything, he goes to the opposite extreme from which he started; all initiative for good is destroyed and the gifts of God remain unused. St. Paul advises parents not to overwhelm their children with rebukes, lest they become weaklings with no heart for anything. This same recommendation must be made to spiritual directors, religious superiors, masters of novices, and those engaged in education. To form souls, one must correct them temperately and moderately.

Consider again someone of poor character, with many flaws in his behavior, but who does try hard to improve. If improperly advised, this sort of person will go to the opposite extreme, becoming now not good but sugary. In his new condition he lacks the firmness to persevere in good and the energy to resist evil. He lacks balance.

Or take somebody else who desires to practice the counsel of poverty, whether in the religious life or in the world. There is danger that he will think of poverty not as generosity in giving but as stinginess in retaining. Now in fact, nothing is so opposed to the spirit of poverty as is miserliness; mean and base as it is, miserliness constitutes avarice in its very worst form. Between extravagance and stinginess there is a just middle ground. A balanced spirituality discovers it.

Finally, consider someone who has ceased to live according to his own taste. Having determined to set aside the natural inclinations toward a good table and fine clothes, he may so give himself to excessive corporal mortification that he ruins his health. Then he begins to take such precautions with regard to himself that by another route he returns to a more refined type of self-indulgence than that which he left. And it all happens for lack of balance.

What happens in the conduct of individual souls is also reflected in the general march of the Church through the centuries. There is a well-known principle of mechanics that every action produces an equal and opposite reaction. The principle seems to hold in the spiritual order as well. The sanctification of souls results from the combined action of God and man. God has the principal role by means of grace; and man the secondary, although necessary, role, which consists in correspondence with grace.

For lack of balance, men have oscillated between two extremes in the twenty centuries of the Church's history. There has been a chain of actions and reactions. Either such importance has been given to the action of grace as practically to suppress the cooperation of man, or else in the attempt to safeguard human liberty, the part of God has been almost suppressed. In the time of St. Augustine, Pelagius and his followers inclined to this latter extreme, even going so far as to affirm that man could save himself by himself, without the help of grace. In order to combat this error, and with his own peculiar fire and eloquence, St. Augustine insisted on the necessity of grace and the gratuitous character of predestination, not perhaps without some danger of excessively belittling man. In the singular struggle between these two tendencies, "Augustinianism" presented in living color the havoc wrought in man by Original Sin and the weakness of man's will agitated as it is by his passions. It affirmed gratuitous predestination, exalting the role of the divine activity, and not always with due moderation.

In the Middle Ages, Augustinianism held sway, especially when St. Thomas Aquinas presented it in a carefully reasoned and serene way. But not all stayed within reasonable and orthodox limits. The "Predestinationism" of Gottschalk went to the point of heresy, and such exaggeration culminated in the errors of Luther, Calvin, Baius, and Jansen.

From the very time of Augustine there was a contrary reaction. After Pelagianism there came Semi-Pelagianism, which, without denying the necessity of grace, affirmed that the first movement of a man toward his conversion comes from man himself, not from God. In the last analysis, it is man himself who decides his own salvation or damnation. Along with this unorthodox reaction, there were also reactions within the bounds of orthodoxy. These gave a special importance to the cooperation of man with God's grace—whether safeguarding sufficiently the rights of God, it is difficult to say. Likewise, "Christian humanism" tried to favor human liberty and give more place to the intervention of man. In order to do this, it abandoned the doctrine of St. Augustine and St. Thomas.

At the end of the sixteenth century, the controversy between these two tendencies became accentuated in the controversy between Báñez and Molina. There arose the two great schools, Thomism and Molinism, whose dramatic struggles so embroiled our theological forebears. Molinism was very successful toward the end of the sixteenth century and during the seventeenth. But it soon provoked reactions, one orthodox, that of the Berullian school or the Oratory, and the other heterodox, that of Jansenism, the second doing as much harm as the first did good.

The Berullian school insisted on "the nothingness of man and the all of God." Beginning with this consideration, it aimed at fostering a proper attitude on the part of man toward God, an attitude of respect and adoration, culminating in love. A major benefit that we owe to this spirituality is a more profound understanding of the mystery of Christ, the incarnate Word. Besides the Sulpicians, St. Vincent de Paul, St. John Eudes, St. John Baptist de la Salle, Fr. Faber, Cardinal Newman, and Msgr. Gay were illustrious representatives of this school.

The Jansenists carried the reaction against Molinism and humanism to its furthest extreme. They boasted of their great severity and asserted that not only one or the other school but the whole Church had departed from the Christian austerity of the first centuries. They exaggerated the corruption caused in human nature by Original Sin and affirmed that the will is wholly inert in the face of evil or good, grace constraining man to do good. They forged a God of whom one could only be afraid, a God who was not a father but a harsh and rigorous master. They affirmed that Jesus Christ had not come to save all men but only the elect. Instead of encouraging the reception of the sacraments, they drew the faithful away from them, especially Confession and Communion, and demanded for their reception a superhuman perfection.

The Jansenists claimed that we are responsible not only for our voluntary actions but for all the acts of our corrupted nature, even involuntary or inadvertent ones. In a word, they turned the whole spiritual life into penance, penance, and more penance. By this excessive stress on penance, they sought to assure their own salvation, for according to them the number of the saved is very small. Having a veritable horror of anything connected with the senses, they did not approve of devotion to the Blessed Virgin or even to the sacred humanity of Jesus Christ, and they looked unkindly on vocal prayers. Their piety was wholly dry, arid, austere, and rigorous—more likely to engender despair than hope.

The severity of the Jansenists produced at the end of the seventeenth century a reaction still more dangerous: quietism. From about the middle of the seventeenth century onward, people began to speak and write a great deal about pure or disinterested love. This was a reaction against the Jansenists, for whom the spiritual life was nothing but severity and fear. The doctrine of pure love led logically to the doctrine of absolute abandonment to the will of

God. This can undoubtedly be understood correctly enough, and the first who spoke on it, men like Nouet, Surin, and de Canfield, did understand it correctly. But little by little, distortions crept in, and finally the genuine quietism of Miguel Molinos.

The false doctrine of quietism teaches that pure love and abandonment to God ought to be carried to an absolute disinterest even in one's own salvation, and that true prayer leads the soul to total passivity and complete inertia. True piety is the total annihilation of the faculties of the soul. The faculties ought to become not only inactive but even inert. The soul ought to become like a corpse, the activity of God taking the place of one's own activity. This is the "mystical death" through which the soul becomes so deified that it constitutes one thing with God. At this point it can no longer sin, even venially.

The soul's inertia excludes discursive prayer and devout reflection. One must not think of Heaven, Hell, or eternity. One must neither be concerned about one's own salvation nor disturbed at the sight of personal faults. Examination of conscience is useless. Devotion to the saints, to the Blessed Virgin, and even to the humanity of Christ must be discarded. And even in the most violent temptations one is not to offer any resistance. It is easy to understand how these errors led in practice to lamentable excesses. Molinos, after being condemned by the Holy Office in 1687, appears to have died repentant.

Perhaps the most striking phase of this struggle involves the two great French ecclesiastics, Bossuet and Fenelon. The controversy between them turned especially around the notion of "pure love." Fenelon affirmed that it was of the essence of perfect charity to love God for His own sake with no relation to our own blessedness. Bossuet, for his part, affirmed that the idea of heavenly reward does not cause charity to be "interested" or selfish, "since the recompense which it desires is no other than He whom it loves, and it does not ask honor nor riches nor pleasures nor any of the other goods which He is able to give but only God Himself."

In order to defend his ideas, Fenelon wrote his book, *The Explanation of the Maxims of the Saints.* In it, as the title indicates, he undertook to explain the experiences and expressions of the saints regarding the interior life, showing that all the interior roads tend to pure or disinterested love. But he failed to give to all these expressions due exactness and precision, so that a kind of mitigated quietism resulted, the fundamental principle of which was a habitual state of pure love in which the desire for reward and the fear of punishment would have no part.

On March 12, 1699, the Holy See condemned Fenelon's book, and on April 9, Fenelon published a pastoral letter in which he declared that he submitted wholly, absolutely, and without restrictions to the judgment of the Church. Even more than the triumph of Bossuet, one must admire the humble and generous submission of Fenelon, who though he erred, "erred," as someone has said, "through love." The truth is that real charity includes the virtue of hope; and however perfect charity may be, it cannot be exclusive of beatitude or the possession of God.

The false mysticism of quietism could not but do harm to true mysticism. As a result, eighteenth-century spiritual authors did not dare to treat of mysticism or even so much as mention it. Almost all confined themselves to treating of asceticism and of the exercise of the moral virtues. There arose the tendency in writers, preachers, and spiritual directors to be purely "practical." Frequently this turned into a kind of casuistry or spiritual empiricism. And yet nothing is more necessary in spirituality than to know the basic principles or fundamental truths, and afterward to apply them to practice. Without grounding in principles, we expose ourselves to serious errors.

Always providential with His Church, God raised up at this time St. Margaret Mary Alacoque and by means of her showed men the treasures hidden in His Heart. This was a magnificent proof that there is a true mysticism and that the rigorism of the Jansenists was false. Later, God's providence gave St. Alphonsus Liguori to the Church, to continue the reaction against the rigorism that was still wreaking havoc. Truly the doctor of prayer, St. Alphonsus found in prayer the secret for resolving in a practical way the terrible problem of predestination: "He who prays will certainly be saved; he who does not pray will certainly be condemned." St. Alphonsus also put new life into devotion to the Holy Eucharist and to the Blessed Virgin.

Finally, toward the end of the nineteenth century, there began a movement of renewal on behalf of mysticism, in which Goerres, Arintero, Meynard, Gardeil, Saudreau, Lamballe, Joret, and Garrigou-Lagrange merit places of honor. Meanwhile the liturgy, forgotten and unknown as far as the simple faithful were concerned, began to see a resurgence, initiated especially by Dom Gueranger, who did so great a service for the Christian people.

This quick historical survey enables us to see the constant fluctuations of the human intelligence, ceaselessly oscillating from extreme to extreme. How rightly does Scripture say, "For the thoughts of mortal men are fearful, and our counsels uncertain" (Wisd. 9:14). Here is where the teaching role of the Supreme Pontiff stands out. Just as the pilot constantly holds the ship in its true course while the waves ceaselessly work to swerve it to the right or to the left, so the teaching authority of the Holy See declares and determines through the centuries what precisely is the truth and ceaselessly corrects the errors of human opinions as they veer from extreme to extreme.

Rule 3

Now what is this oscillation but a lack of balance? How rare it is to find someone who is completely balanced in his judgments. All of us, to quote St. Paul, are like "children, tossed to and fro and carried about by every wind of doctrine devised in the wickedness of men, in craftiness, according to the wiles of error" (Eph. 4:14). We see everything in terms of our own ego. We are influenced by our own temperament, which in some is violent and impulsive, in others impressionable and susceptible, in others indolent, lazy, inert. Personality traits affect our way of looking at things; some are naturally optimistic and see everything through rose-colored glasses, while others pessimistically incline to judge every cause as already lost. Personal interest and love of self cause us to judge truth to be where convenience is; we will not hear of our own opinions being criticized and insist on our own judgment being right against every wind and tide. Finally, our passions blind us, or at the very least obscure the true and the right.

How are we to achieve that all-important balance of outlook and activity? Without any question the road is long, and the work is the work of a lifetime. But we have basic principles to guide us. First, God made man a rational being and intends man to be guided by his reason. Second, in the present order man must direct his actions not by reason alone but by reason elevated and illumined by faith. We must therefore work to get rid of the obstacles that obstruct the clear vision of reason and faith. And we must make positive use of reason enlightened by faith to direct our whole life, interior and exterior. We must work, then, to moderate the excesses of our temperament and to supply for its deficiencies. We must correct our character defects; we must gain dominion over our passions. In brief, we have to strangle our egoism.

Above all, we must act as rational beings, and we must live by faith. The task assigned to us is to elevate ourselves above the meanness of our passions, the inconstancy of passing impressions, the fickleness of feeling. We are to elevate ourselves to that serene and pure region where in silence and peace everything is seen from the point of view of God, His interests, His glory, His love. We will work as those who belong not to time but to eternity. We will regard ourselves not as permanent settlers who have established their patrimony here but as travelers passing by in search of another and eternal homeland. Only by viewing things in this light can we have perfect balance.

Rule 4

We must learn to love and to practice every kind of humiliation.

Everybody is aware of the truly basic character of humility at every turn of the spiritual life. The more one advances in the practice of virtue, the more permeated must he be with humility. The most elevated heights of perfection suppose unsounded abysses of humility. St. Augustine teaches us this graphically. The higher the building you propose to construct, he says, the deeper you must dig your foundation. The higher the building of our perfection, the deeper must be the foundations of humility.

Supernatural humility is an infused virtue put into the soul by God as part of the whole retinue of moral virtues that accompany sanctifying grace. Nevertheless, in order to be preserved, grow, and acquire the facility proper to the acquired virtues, infused humility must be exercised, just as must the other supernatural virtues. Now the acts proper to humility, or the occasions that give opportunity to exercise it, are *humiliations*. This is why our fourth rule speaks not directly of humility but of humiliations. Now, although we speak of humiliations, it would be an error to try to acquire humility by external acts alone. Like all virtues, humility springs from a light.

This light is a supernatural one, which manifests to us our own helplessness, nothingness, and misery.

The rule says that we must practice every kind of humiliation. What kinds of humiliation are there? We can consider three: those that come from ourselves or that we voluntarily seek out; those that come from men; and those that come from God.

Much discretion is needed in order not to fall into lamentable exaggerations when there is question of seeking humiliation on our own. Someone who lacks balance or good practical judgment, or who does not subject himself to his director in such matters, will make not only himself but also virtue look ridiculous. This is what happens when under the guise of practicing humility, a person assumes an affected and shrunken demeanor, eyes cast down, head lowered, hands folded, and goes about affirming in season and out of season that he is worthless, a great sinner, of no use whatsoever. A few think to exercise humility by dressing carelessly and wearing worn-out, dirty, or outlandish clothes. And some will deliberately do badly that which they have been commanded to do, in order to win a rebuke.

In doing such things one runs the risk of fostering secret pride instead of practicing humility. We expose ourselves to vain complacency in our pretended virtue, or at the very least to a kind of false humility, because by these external humiliations we may be at least unconsciously trying to acquire or sustain a reputation for virtue and holiness. The humiliations we can safely seek of our own choice are those that go unperceived. For example, we can avoid speaking of ourselves where there is no real need for doing so. We can practice exterior modesty and avoid excessive forwardness, not to say impertinence. We can avoid ostentation in clothing, living quarters, and furnishings. Besides often being in bad taste, this serves for nothing but to encourage vanity and to waste money that could be given to help the poor. We can observe moderation in discussions, avoiding real arguments whenever possible and never maintaining our own opinion acrimoniously. If we have authority, we can issue orders without causing the weight of authority to be felt. We can reprimand only when this is absolutely necessary and truly for the good of souls. A reproof ought to be a light that enables a person at fault to see his error, not an insult that wounds, nor a mere outburst of anger.

Second, there are humiliations that come to us from others. Since they arise from the will of another, our only task is to bear them with patience, or better, to accept them calmly and serenely. Such a humiliation may occur when we are rebuked without reason, or when we are criticized unjustly or falsely. To bear these humiliations without getting upset, we should remember that we are bad judges in what touches ourselves and our own innocence or guilt. Supposing that we are truly innocent in some particular instance, how many other times have we really been at fault and no one reproved us! It is merely a matter of confusion of dates! Whenever we are falsely accused, we ought to dwell upon our real but hidden faults, reminding ourselves that the truth will come out sooner or later and that "God speaks through him who keeps silent." Sometimes humiliations occur when our superiors fail to give us certain considerations that we should like to receive but that we are, in fact, very far from deserving. A superior keeps us waiting overlong, refuses to give us a hearing, speaks to us gruffly or harshly. We should remember that God permits such things precisely to give us another opportunity to practice virtue. We might keep in mind the Canaanite woman whom our Lord treated with harsh words, but only to move her to such virtue that He Himself exclaimed, "O woman, great is thy faith!" (Matt. 15:21-28).

We might, too, have some pity on poor superiors, besieged as they are day and night. There comes a point at which human resistance reaches its limit, at which from sheer physical exhaustion a person is not equal to a smile. A superior's physique does not yet have the endowments that come with glorification.

Humiliations may also come when those who are subject to us do not give us quite the attention and consideration we think we deserve. They may not run the roll call of all the honorific titles that we think belong to us. They may fail to serve and obey us with quite the submission of slaves. Well, let us remember that our subjects are not properly our inferiors. True worth does not depend on the particular office a person discharges. God is the true judge of personal worth. Before Him many a superior will be inferior to some of his subjects.

Humiliations come, too, when justifiably or unjustifiably the office that we exercise is taken away from us and we have to descend to the common level. It is extremely difficult to step gracefully up into some new and higher responsibility. But it would appear almost impossible to step gracefully down from it. Those are able to step down gracefully from some position who through personal gifts and virtue are actually superior to the particular duty entrusted to them. In the case of such persons, the duty or position really becomes a pedestal from which their personal worth stands out better. Those who cannot step gracefully into some higher post are inferior to it. The position subjects them to itself; they try to use the position to make up for their own personal mediocrity and lack of virtue. But if stepping up is hard, stepping down is harder. How rare is the person who steps down gracefully, who descends naturally, without loss of peace, and with equanimity and serenity! Only the saints do it. There can hardly be a surer proof of profound humility and lofty perfection than to step down well from a lofty post to an insignificant one.

Superiors have been known to humiliate their subjects deliberately to teach them humility. Those having the responsibility of forming souls—spiritual directors, masters of novices, religious superiors, educators, fathers of families—sometimes try to make their subjects humble by dint of trumped-up humiliations. With the talented they find fault at every turn as fools and idiots. They exaggerate the faults of those who have acquired some virtue and reprimand them publicly. They ridicule unmercifully those who have artistic ability.

What are we to say of such a system? Far from forming humble souls, it is likely to have one of the following results. First, it may produce wounded and hurt, weak and cowardly individuals; as a result of being told that they are good for nothing they come to believe it and become completely useless. Or such a system turns out persons full of silent rebellion and secret pride. Injustice produces stubbornness. The abused person begins to reason, "If they so humble me, it is because I am worth so much." No, you cannot make souls humble with a big stick.

Finally, there are the humiliations that come from God. Some of these come indirectly from God and others directly. When God desires that we know our misery from personal experience, He may permit not only temptations but real falls. To cure pride, for example, which is a kind of spiritual lust, He may permit falls in matters of purity.

The humiliations that come directly from God are at bottom a kind of light, though at first they may not seem so. God does not humble us as creatures do, by blows. He simply illuminates our soul so that it may comprehend in a supernatural way its nothingness and misery. God humbles by illuminating. He enables us to understand something of His own grandeur, perfection, and holiness. By sheer contrast we understand as never before our nothingness and misery and would like some deep hole in which to bury ourselves.

We cannot possess a profound humility until the gifts of the Holy Spirit come into play: the gift of fear of the Lord, which inspires in us a deep and reverential fear; the gift of piety, which makes us venerate God as our Father; the gift of knowledge, which makes us understand the vanity of everything created, of every dignity and honor; and especially the gift of understanding, which makes us penetrate somewhat into the all that God is and the nothing that the creature is. By the gift of understanding we can appreciate that incomparable little dialogue between God and St. Catherine of Siena:

"Do you know what it is that you are and what it is that I am?"

"No, Lord, not unless You tell me."

"Very well; you are she who is not, and I am He who is."

We all know this truth theoretically. But what a different knowledge we can have of it when God makes it divinely known, His dazzling light illuminating the inmost recesses of our intelligence. We are left emptied of self and free of pride. We want neither high temporal honors nor striking spiritual graces with which we may impress others.

Such are the various kinds of humiliation. Our rule in fact demands more than their mere practice. We ought not only to practice humiliation but to *love* it. Is it possible to love humiliation? If humiliation be considered only in itself, certainly not. But if we take into account that humiliation is the absolutely indispensable condition of God's lowering Himself to the soul, enriching it with His highest graces and lavishing upon it the most wonderful gifts of His love—is not humiliation then made lovable? Someone has said that "at the bottom of humiliations accepted one finds peace." And so it is. For in humiliations one finds God. The Blessed Virgin knew this better than anyone else. As she herself explained, "He has regarded the lowliness of His handmaid; for, behold, henceforth all generations shall call me blessed.... He who is mighty has done great things for me, and holy is His name" (Luke 1:48–49).

Rule 5

We must come to realize that sanctity is not achieved in one leap but only through a very slow and gradual ascent; it generally starts from very insignificant beginnings.

It is a law of divine providence, in the distribution of graces and the sanctification of souls, that the higher the sanctity to which a soul is destined, the more humble and hidden are its beginnings. Most of us, nevertheless, are not prepared for this way of acting on God's part. Our judgment has been warped by lives of the saints written without historical sense and with an exaggerated eagerness to edify. These books hide the defects of the saints, speak only of their virtues, and place too much emphasis on extraordinary things. The saints appear not as human beings, weak and full of misery like the rest of us, but as extraordinary and privileged beings of a different order. Instead of being spurred to imitate them, we find ourselves disillusioned and discouraged.

Poets, it is said, are "born, not made." A person who does not have the poetic gift will never succeed in becoming a real poet even if he studies all his life. And, on the other hand, a person born with a natural gift might never study and yet compose verse of merit, even though not wholly in accord with the rules of poetic composition. Exactly the opposite must be said of saints: They are "made, not born." St. Augustine's assertion that "He who made you without yourself will not save you without yourself" applies with special force to sanctity. He who made you without yourself will certainly not *sanctify* you without yourself. Holiness is always the fruit of grace on the part of God, and of the correspondence with grace on the part of man.

It is an error both theological and historical to think that saints were just born saints. True, this is what some hagiographers would have us believe. According to them, the saint at the moment of birth found himself enveloped in a mysterious light; in order to celebrate his birth, the bells rang out even with no one to ring them. Now, even supposing the historical truth of such extraordinary events, it is of paramount importance to insist that sanctity does not consist in them. Such incidents, in fact, neither particularly edify nor move to imitation. Individuals who pay too much attention to them either become discouraged or fall into self-deceit.

Theologians call such extraordinary favors "graces gratuitously given" (*gratiae gratis datae*) because they are not given to a soul to sanctify it, as is the "grace that makes pleasing" (*gratia gratum faciens*), but rather for the profit and advantage of others. They give accreditation to a mission or convince men of the sanctity of someone when such fits in with the plans of God.

True sanctity ordinarily has very small beginnings. At first it is hidden, almost insignificant. It develops so gradually that it almost always passes unnoticed, not only by the world at large but even by those who could be firsthand witnesses to it. The last to notice it are the saints themselves. Sanctity is the seed hidden in the furrow of the soul, a seed at first seen by none and that germinates slowly. First a tender, tiny shoot bursts forth. Gradually developing, it finally becomes a great tree where the birds of the air come for refuge and in whose shade the tired traveler takes shelter.

Sanctity is like the light of day, which begins so imperceptibly that we cannot say exactly when night ends and day begins. The diffused semi-light increases little by little until it finally becomes the soft light of the dawn that precedes the rising of the sun. At length, the sun appears, its light warm and mild and soft. As it rises more and more above the horizon, the light and heat increase until with the arrival of high noon there is a veritable flood of light and a furnace of heat. Sanctity is like a river. When we watch the river emptying into the ocean, the volume of its waters is so great that it appears one thing with the ocean. But if we follow the current back, we see that the river is formed by various tributaries; and if we follow it to its origin, we find hardly more than a tiny trickle.

Sanctity is the delicate trace of light that cannot be completely distinguished from the shadows of the night but that increases and increases until it is transformed into the full day of eternity. Sanctity is the trickle of water that grows through life until it becomes the abundant river that goes on to lose itself in the immense ocean of God.

Why does sanctity grow so gradually? Sanctity is at bottom nothing but the life of grace. And this life, like all life, begins from a seed that must develop in order to reach full growth. Except for the infinite and immutable life of God, all life, both natural and supernatural, is subject to development. Like a seed, it comes to maturity only by degrees. God does not forge saints all at once, as one might cast a medal. God's making of a saint is rather like the work of an artist who, taking a piece of marble, little by little cuts and polishes and chisels until he has turned it into a beautiful statue. But there is a difference; the block of marble is entirely passive, while man must cooperate in the work of sanctification.

That the saints do not happen all at once can be verified from experience. Francis of Assisi was very far from being born a saint.

As a child he lived like other children. As a young man he was no different from many others. He was indeed endowed with an exceedingly sensitive nature, and being overmuch given to sensible things, he liked to dress well, sit down to a fine table, play the guitar, and sing. He took part in parties with his friends. He was, if anything, quite conspicuous at every party, the most hilarious and noisiest of all. If at this time someone had prophetically told him that he was one day to be a canonized saint or that he would soon be going about dressed in a robe of rough wool tied with a crude cord, he would have burst out laughing: "And these, I suppose, are the signs?"

How did the sanctity of Francis Bernardone, the poor man of Assisi, begin? With something very ordinary and trivial. One day he met a beggar who asked for alms. He kept on going, but then touched by the grace of the Holy Spirit, he turned back and gave the man some help. Francis responded to grace and had the satisfaction of having done a good turn and alleviated someone's misery. This little spark of generosity was the beginning of a holocaust of charity.

How grace adapts itself to nature! Francis was of a nature generous to the point of wastefulness. He began to hand out money on all sides and with lavish hands. His alarmed father finally accused him before the bishop of squandering his property. Not out of spite but because he could no longer hold himself back from the way of complete detachment, Francis handed over to his father everything, right down to the expensive clothes he had on his back. Then he came to know not only the satisfaction of doing good but also the sublime happiness of calling God his Father. God had been but waiting to see the heart of Francis empty. He at once began to fill it with a love that would bring it eventually to the seraphic transfiguration of La Verna. A sanctity so elevated with beginnings so insignificant! How many times we have met the needy only to pass them by? Or perhaps we have helped them and yet still have not begun the road to sanctity!

What is true of St. Francis can be verified in other saints. The holiness of St. Ignatius, the founder of the Jesuits, had equally humble beginnings. In order to divert himself while laid up in the hospital, he looked about for something to read. There fell into his hands two books, one about Christ and another about Christ's saints. To kill time, and purely out of curiosity, he began to read. And he was on his way to sanctity! The holiness of Francis Xavier, the apostle to India, whose arms grew weary from innumerable Baptisms, began its wonderful course when St. Ignatius repeated to him the sentence from the Gospel: "What does it profit a man to gain the whole world, if he suffer the loss of his own soul?" St. Francis Borgia, St. Silvester, and St. Bruno are said to have begun their conversions by contemplating a corpse.

How many times have we read the lives of the saints, or heard snatches of the Gospels, or looked upon the bodies of the deceased! Yet have we even begun to be saints? If St. Francis had not corresponded with grace on that particular occasion, would he have frustrated his sanctification? And what of the other saints? If they had not corresponded with that first little grace, would they have become saints?

Before we try to answer, let us consider the truly enormous consequences that go with a soul's becoming holy or not becoming holy. If Luther had corresponded with grace, he would have remained faithful to his calling. The world might have escaped one of the worst heresies in history. Millions, whole nations through centuries, would not have been separated from Christ's Church. Can we calculate the loss of souls occasioned by the infidelity to grace of Martin Luther?

The holiness of St. Francis of Assisi, St. Ignatius Loyola, St. John Bosco, St. Margaret Mary, and the Little Flower, was tied in by God with the salvation and sanctification of innumerable other persons. If they had not become saints, many others would not have reached sanctity and many might have been lost.

Here we touch upon the great mystery of the solidarity of souls, which at bottom is but the dogma of the communion of saints. In the supernatural order, nobody lives in isolation. In a greater or lesser degree, one person influences others, so that nobody is saved alone and nobody is lost alone.

In particular, there are those who are, as it were, the center of others. We see this in the ecclesiastical hierarchy. The pope is the center of the whole Church, the bishop of a whole diocese. The pastor is a kind of spiritual focal point for his parishioners, the priest for the souls that God has entrusted to him, religious founders for whole religious families, superiors for those in their charge. All holy persons are the center of a multitude of others. The failure of a soul to become holy is a true catastrophe compared with which a world war is like the play of children. And holiness depends on correspondence with a first grace often humble and hidden.

But let us return to our problem: If St. Francis of Assisi had not corresponded with the inspiration to help that particular beggar, would his sanctification have been frustrated and consequently that of countless others? Speaking absolutely, we must answer in the negative. God has too many ways to compensate for a failure, to make up for an infidelity, to correct an error. This is especially true when there is a question of graces that, in appearance at least, are relatively insignificant.

Nevertheless, it seems no exaggeration to affirm that there are infidelities, in appearance small, that make a whole life take a different direction. There are crucial graces. Until some given moment, there is only one road in some particular person's life. But in that given moment, a person arrives at a crossroads. The path divides, and as the person moves along one fork, he gets farther and farther from the other. The destinations of the two are completely different. Perhaps we might say that God has two classes of graces. One class, of the secondary order, He scatters in abundance, taking into account how much will be lost by our lack of correspondence. But He has others that can be called "capital." A grace of this class can be compared to a link of a chain. When a person gets hold of the first link and draws it to himself, the second follows; it in turn draws the third and so on successively until the last. On the other hand, let the first link slip, and the whole chain is gone. Such are the "capital" graces. They constitute, as it were, the substance of the designs of God with regard to some particular person. They are nothing but the mission or vocation of a person to that special degree of sanctity to which God has called him.

Ordinarily, the first link in this chain is very small. Each link is progressively larger until we come to the great link that unites us definitely and forever with God. And if one considers well, these links are not in reality many graces but at bottom only one grace that develops as a living seed develops into a plant.

Be these things as they may, the result of our reflections cannot be less than this: correspondence with grace is of crucial importance. Those little graces, the little inspirations that we treat lightly because they are small, may well be the seed of a holy life. "Well done, good and faithful servant; because thou hast been faithful over a few things, I will set thee over many" (Matt. 25:21). Our Lord need not be understood as meaning only that our tiny good works receive from God a huge reward of eternal happiness. He may also mean that a person who corresponds with little graces will receive greater, progressively greater ones, until he reaches the summit of perfection. The secret of sanctity is fidelity to grace, correspondence with the very slightest inspirations of the Holy Spirit.

Rule 6

We must learn to pray and to mortify ourselves out of love.

This rule comes very fittingly after our earlier discussion of humility. Prayer springs up spontaneously from the depths of humiliation. "Out of the depths I have cried to Thee, O Lord" (Ps. 129:1). It is as if the Psalmist would say, "From the depths of *humiliation*, O Lord, I have cried to Thee."

Pride is unable to pray. How unbearably proud was the unbeliever who advised, "Do not kneel. You are already small enough. Don't make yourself still smaller by kneeling." This advice comes naturally from the lips of a proud man. To pray, one must feel one's need, and the proud man thinks that he is sufficient to himself.

The first kind of prayer is that of the beggar, who, because he is hungry, extends his hand to ask for a piece of bread. St. Augustine says, "You are God's beggar. All of us are mendicants of God when we pray. We stand before the door of the great father of the family. We prostrate ourselves on our knees, begging for something. That something is God Himself. What does the beggar ask of you? Bread. And what do you ask of God? Why, that He give you Christ, who said of Himself: 'I am the living bread that has come down from heaven.'"

Without humility nobody can recognize himself as a beggar, even in the face of God. If prayer begins with asking, it ends in adoring, in that supreme adoration that becomes one thing with unitive love and culminates in the possession of God. To attain to lofty prayer, one must lower himself still more into the abyss of humility. St. Augustine teaches us that we approach God, who is very high, by becoming ourselves very low. God withdraws from the person who proudly raises himself up, and He draws near to one who humbly lowers himself. The loftiest summits of holiness rise up alongside the most profound abysses of humility.

The spiritual life can be almost identified with the life of prayer. In its fullness the spiritual life consists in the union of the soul with God. And the life of prayer also is nothing but the union of the soul with God. There is no better criterion of progress in perfection than prayer. It is impossible to live without breathing. And the necessity that the body has for breathing is the necessity that the soul ought to feel for prayer. Prayer is the respiration of the soul, and without it the soul cannot live.

The role of prayer in the spiritual life can be likened to the role of the heart in a living body. The heart expands in order to receive the flow of blood. Then immediately it contracts, sending the flow of blood to the other organs and flooding them with life. So the soul must expand through prayer in order to receive the flow of graces from Heaven. It can then spread these graces through the whole spiritual organism, and even make them circulate through the whole Mystical Body of Christ.

We set certain definite hours for nourishment, but not for breathing. Breathing fills our whole life. We breathe asleep and awake, at work and at rest, sick and well. Prayer is like breathing in that we ought to pray always. Jesus Christ recommended us to "always pray and not lose heart" (Luke 18:1); therefore, the strength to pray need never be wanting to us.

Someone directed by St. Francis de Sales presented for his approval a daily schedule of spiritual exercises that began with one hour of mental prayer. The saint crossed this out and in its place put twenty-four hours. He wanted to emphasize the truth that prayer is not to be a single exercise in the day but must fill the whole day.

The time dedicated expressly to prayer in any program of the spiritual life ought to signify the period for making "prayer provisions" for the whole day. A hiker getting ready for a long trip loads his knapsack with adequate food supplies. Someone sensitive to cold approaches the stove to warm himself before going into the chilly out-of-doors. So by formal prayer we prepare ourselves for the day. We must strive to make our lives a constant treating with God, in the midst of the occupations, conversations, and difficulties that form the framework of our day. Our lives can be a constant living with God if we but prolong our prayer, or the contact with God that is the fruit of prayer. From time to time, we must freshen our contact by a simple raising of our mind to God or by means of ejaculatory prayers, spiritual communions, interior aspirations.

A person at first will find difficulty in attending at the same time to external occupations and interior union with God. Many times he will surprise himself in the midst of distractions that have taken his thoughts very far from God indeed. But if he is faithful in his efforts, distractions will disappear little by little. He will come to live in a supernatural atmosphere, in constant contact with God, like the fish that lives submerged in water or the eagle that moves in the vastness of space. This is to live a life of prayer, and only when one has arrived at this point has he fully learned to pray.

Mortification is as indispensable as prayer in the spiritual life, granted our state of being sinners. Mortification is necessary for the expiation of past sins and the conquest of present ones. It is required for successful resistance to the inclination to evil left in the soul by Original Sin and strengthened by personal sin. Mortification is necessary not only in the purgative way but also in the illuminative. We cannot imitate Jesus crucified without carrying in our own flesh the sacred marks of Jesus' Passion. "I bear the marks of the Lord Jesus in my body" (Gal. 6:17). Mortification is necessary even in the unitive way in order that, uniting our sufferings with those of our Savior, we may continue His redemptive work, obtaining graces of conversion for sinners and graces of sanctification for the just. In this way we complete, on behalf of Christ's Mystical Body, the Church, "what is lacking of the sufferings of Christ" (Col. 1:24).

One kind of mortification may be more valuable than another. Mortifications that come from God, like sickness, poverty, failure, and humiliation, are worth more than those like fasting that come from our own will. Interior mortification—patience in bearing with one's neighbor, refusing to indulge one's own bad disposition, avoiding making excuses when reprimanded—this is of more value than exterior or bodily mortifications. But no one should limit himself to one kind of mortification. The different kinds can be combined. Mortification on our own initiative will help us to receive properly the mortifications that come to us from others, and ultimately from God. In the same way, corporal mortification will help us in the practice of interior mortification. And all prudent mortification will dispose us for union with God.

Prayer and mortification—what is the connection that exists between them? So profound a connection that St. John of the Cross declares, "Tell me what your mortification is like, and I will tell you what your prayer is like." Prayer consists in union with God. But we unite ourselves with God in the measure in which we purify ourselves, for nothing impure can be united with infinite purity. Now, the great instrument for obtaining purity of soul is mortification. Just as fire purifies gold, so mortification purifies the soul, burning all the dross and remains of sin and preparing the soul for union with God.

God is an infinitely exalted being, and prayer is a lifting up of the mind and heart to Him. The soul, being spiritual, tends of itself to rise. But the weight of human miseries is a ballast that drags it toward the earth and makes its ascension difficult. Mortification destroys the attraction of the corporeal. It cuts the moorings of the human and earthly and frees the soul for a heavenly ascent.

Perfect union requires the perfect likeness of the things united. Now, St. Paul tells us we ought not to know any other Christ than Christ crucified. But we cannot unite ourselves to such a Christ if we do not by mortification crucify ourselves, so that with the same apostle we can say, "With Christ I am nailed to the Cross" (Gal. 2:19).

Finally, the life of prayer, like all life, must be fruitful. The most intense and fruitful apostolate is exercised by those who pray. But fruitfulness in prayer is achieved when the soul, not only united with Christ but transformed into Him, comes to be an instrument or, as it were, a prolongation of the humanity of Christ. Through such a soul Christ continues His Passion and sacrifice, His work of redemption and sanctification. But to share with Christ in this way one must mortify oneself through love and love alone. This is why St. John of the Cross said with good reason, "Tell me what your mortification is like, and I will tell you what your prayer is like." And this is why our sixth rule exhorts us "to pray and to mortify ourselves out of love."

Rule 7

We must learn that it is not consolation but adversity that brings us close to God and unites us to Him.

In order to understand this rule, we must first grasp the meaning of *consolation* and *adversity*. Naturally we are speaking of consolation and adversity in the service of God. But tying in this seventh rule more particularly with the sixth, which treats of prayer, we have in mind here especially consolation and adversity in prayer or conversation with God.

By consolation we understand all those delights that may be found in prayer. These may be purely sensible, purely spiritual, or spiritual and sensible at one and the same time. We must keep in mind that there are two kinds of knowing powers in man: the senses, by means of which we perceive the sensible; and the intellect, by means of which we know intelligible truth. Likewise, there are two kinds of powers for loving the good: the sensible appetites, which seek the sensible good manifested through the senses; and the will, which loves immaterial good presented through the intellect.

Every faculty seeks its own proper good. When it has found that good and possesses it, there results the delight that we call joy. If the good is sensible, the joy is sensible; if the good is immaterial, the joy is immaterial. Sensible consolations here refer to the joy or delight that we experience in our sense powers when we pray to God. This joy resides in the sense faculties, or, in the language of the Scholastics, in the concupiscible appetite. Sensible joy has sensible manifestations. For example, the cheeks become flushed, tears flow, the heart palpitates, or even the whole body trembles. Spiritual consolation is the joy or delight the will experiences in the possession of the good proper to it. Spiritual consolation resides in the will and does not itself have sensible manifestations.

Finally, because of the union of soul with body and the mutual influence exercised by each upon the other, when spiritual consolation is abundant it overflows the spiritual part of the soul and floods the inferior part of our being or our sensible nature. The Psalmist expressed this fullness of consolation when he said, "My heart and my flesh have rejoiced in the living God" (Ps. 83:3). Not only my heart (my will) but even my flesh itself has trembled with joy.

Purely sensible consolations belong especially to beginners; purely spiritual ones, to the proficient or those who are progressing in the way of perfection; and the integral consolations, spiritual and sensible, are characteristic of the perfect. We speak here in a predominating sense, not in an exclusive one. The three stages of the spiritual life are the purgative, proper to beginners; the illuminative, belonging to proficients; and the unitive, belonging to the perfect. Now, each of the three kinds of consolation appears in each stage of the spiritual life. But the purely spiritual predominates in the illuminative way, and the complete or integral in the unitive way.

We can set up this general rule: a person must not become attached to consolations, especially sensible ones; he must make use of them as a pure means for getting to God. To become attached to consolations, to want them inordinately, to seek them as an end and not as a means, is a spiritual vice St. John of the Cross calls "spiritual gluttony." But this does not mean that one would be justified in systematically despising them. Whenever God sends them, He sends them for our spiritual profit.

It will now be easier to understand what we mean by adversity in prayer. It is simply the absence of consolations. More particularly, it can be called aridity, impotence, desolation, abandonment. And these terms may well be used to signify adversity in its varying degrees.

The lack of sensible consolation we call aridity. Aridity deprives one of the sensible delight previously tasted in prayer. As the sensible part of the soul now finds no nourishment, the result of aridity is distractions. The imagination, finding nothing on which to feed in prayer, readily begins to roam and to occupy itself with other than spiritual things.

A further degree of trial in prayer is impotence. A person not only lacks fervor and sensible devotion. He further feels himself impotent even for acts of the higher faculties, reflection on the part of the intellect and affections on the part of the will.

A yet higher degree is desolation. Over and above the experience of impotence, a person finds in spiritual things nothing but weariness, tediousness, and repugnance.

Last of all there is abandonment. This is the last and greatest trial that the soul can suffer in prayer. Not only does one here find spiritual things repugnant, but he feels himself abandoned by God. He is shaken by temptations against faith, and all spiritual things appear to be a farce. Temptations against hope work to convince him that he is reprobate, already lost. Temptations against love bring horrible blasphemies to his lips. He even appears to hate God.

These states of adversity in prayer must be carefully distinguished from lukewarmness. Lukewarmness, too, can produce aridity, impotence, and weariness in prayer. But lukewarmness is characterized by a willful and habitual negligence. Careless about his spiritual obligations, the lukewarm person abuses grace and nourishes affection for venial sin. The spiritual states referred to above are characterized by the continuance and increase of impotence *in spite of the efforts of the soul against it.* In addition, they are accompanied by an emptiness and disenchantment as far as creatures are concerned, a divine uneasiness and restlessness, a hunger and thirst for God, which already constitutes a kind of obscure contemplation or infused knowledge of God. In this obscurity, the soul knows God as one might know the magnitude of the ocean by the abyss that would be left upon the withdrawal of its waters, or as a person realizes how much he has loved someone through the emptiness left by death.

If both adversity and consolation have a part to play in our sanctification, what is the relative value of each?

First, as to their causes, sensible consolation and bitterness can come from a person's temperament. There are highly sensitive and emotional temperaments that react to the slightest stimulation. Then there are the extraordinarily dry or "melancholy" temperaments—those who, as St. John of the Cross says, seem scarcely to have sufficient sensibility to remain human. Moreover, difficulty in prayer is sometimes temporary and can arise from illness—for example, poor digestion, improper glandular function, or nervous depression.

Sensible consolations sometimes come from the devil. He may try to arouse sensible "devotion" in us in order to deceive us into taking for solid progress in prayer what is really but a sentimental and passing fervor. Or he may use sensible sweetness as a means to start souls on the tragically perilous path of false mysticism.

Sensible consolations also come from God. How often are men drawn away from virtue by the fascination of sensible creatures!

It is natural that, knowing our nature so well, God should make use of the purely sensible to draw us also to His service. This is why beginners in prayer are frequently favored with a period of great sensible fervor. Beginners are like children. They like nothing but sweets, and even when giving them medicine, God hides it in caramels and chocolates.

Consolations and adversity that involve more than the sensible part of human nature can come only from God. Purely spiritual consolations, and above all those spiritual consolations that because of their intensity redound into the sensible part, are but God's reward to those who have been generous in enduring aridity, impotence, desolation, and abandonment. These states of soul are as a rule mystical; the soul cannot produce them by its own power, nor can it by its own power cause them to disappear.

The reason for our seventh rule should now be clear. When a person first begins to serve God, sensible devotion helps pull him free of creatures and attach him to God. But once he has become somewhat stable in God's service, God deprives him of these consolations. For these consolations themselves are of the creaturely order, and a man must be free of attachment to them in order to live for God alone. In the process of bringing a soul to Himself, God does two things. He purifies the soul, emptying it of all creatures and of itself; He fills it with grace and charity so as to unite it directly to Him.

The three stages through which one ascends to union with God must be preceded, then, by three purifications. In the purgative way, there is the active purification of the senses; at the threshold of the illuminative way, the passive purification of the senses; at the entrance to the unitive way, the passive purification of intellect and will. Impotence, desolation, and abandonment correspond to these three purifications. And only after one has passed through these three "nights," as St. John of the Cross calls them, does the light of spiritual consolation shine in the heaven of the soul, as a legitimate reward.

According to the ordinary economy of grace, virtue will not be achieved in a heroic degree except by means of these successive privations of consolations, each more trying and more purifying than its predecessor. These privations teach us experimentally our weakness and helplessness. As a solid humility forms in us, we come to realize the necessity of grace and its true value. We acquire that obscure faith St. John of the Cross so extols. We learn to "hope against hope." Attaining that pure unadorned charity that is the death of the most dangerous and subtle of our spiritual defects, self-love, we arrive at the summit of genuine "pure love," perfect conformity of our will with the will of God.

Adversity, then, not sweetness or consolation, leads us near to God and to eventual union with Him. Adversity is the way or road to God, the instrument God uses to unite us to Him. Sweetness or consolation is the fruit of this union. We barely taste of the fruit here on earth; we enjoy it fully in Heaven.

Rule 8

We must so accustom ourselves to the presence of God that we cannot live without looking to Christ at our side.

The preceding rules are concerned with prayer, either preparing for it or treating of it directly. This rule is meant to complete the material touching on prayer. It is concerned with the prolongation of prayer through the day. By the practice of the presence of God, our whole life can be a life of prayer. Let us practice interior recollection.

Along with prayer, spiritual reading, examination of conscience, and frequenting the sacraments, the practice of the presence of God has become a recognized part of the spiritual life. This practice prepares for, accompanies, and follows prayer. It prepares for prayer, because if we live habitually in the presence of God, we will always be recollected; and recollection, exterior and interior, is the principal preparation demanded by prayer. Exterior recollection consists in guarding the senses, by the observance of exterior and interior silence and modesty. Interior recollection consists precisely in the habitual practice of the presence of God.

The exercise of the presence of God accompanies prayer, because one cannot begin to pray without putting oneself in the presence of God. The traditional custom of explicitly putting oneself in the presence of God before meditation is but an acknowledgment of this. If in prayer we are going to talk to God, we must begin by reminding ourselves that we are in His presence, that He sees us, listens to us, and is attentive to our words.

Finally, this exercise is the prolongation of prayer through the whole day, in conformity with the various occupations to which we must devote ourselves.

The exercise of the presence of God has its roots deep in dogma. Of the truths on which it is founded, some pertain to the natural and some to the supernatural order.

A truth of the natural order is that God is present everywhere by what theologians call His immensity and ubiquity. A body is completely circumscribed by the place in which it is. It cannot be in two places at the same time except through a miracle. Such a miracle, verified in the lives of the saints, is called bilocation. But even then the real body is only in one of the two places; there is but the appearance of a body in the other. The angels, being pure spirits, are not circumscribed by one particular place; they can be in two or more places at one and the same time. God, the purest of spirits, not only can be in several places, but He is in fact in all places.

Moreover, God is where He is after the manner of a spirit. Having no parts, He cannot be divided, and He is wholly in the whole universe and wholly in each one of the creatures that make up the universe. God is wholly in the whole ocean and wholly in each drop of water in the ocean. God is wholly in the endless expanses of the universe and wholly in each one of the atoms that compose it. God is therefore wholly in each and every man, the greatest sinner, the worst criminal, and even the damned. The first truth on which my exercise of the presence of God is based is this: God is in me.

Not only is God everywhere. He also knows everything. His knowledge is infinite. It is impossible that there should be anything past, present, or future, anywhere in the universe, to which God's eye does not reach. No one knows as He does the nature, temperament, character, personal habits, thoughts, desires, and intentions of each one of us. God sees all that we have been, are, and will be. Scripture teaches us that everything is patent and manifest to His eyes, and that He searches into the most intimate depths of our being: "But all things are naked and open to the eyes of him to whom we have to give account" (Heb. 4:13); "the wickedness of sinners shall be brought to nought: and thou shalt direct the just: the searcher of hearts and reins is God" (Ps. 7:10). This, then, is the second truth on which the practice of the presence of God is based: God sees me.

But not only is God's knowledge and presence all-pervasive. It is everywhere active. No creature can do anything except under the influence of the divine action and in dependence on the divine action. God is always the primary and principal cause. With respect to God, no creature can be other than a secondary or instrumental cause. Consider the way in which an instrument works. A paintbrush paints. But it is impossible that it do so except under the motion of the painter. A piano plays, but only at the touch of the artist. Now, all creatures are instruments of God. All creation is an immense lyre played by the divine hands.

This truth applies even to man, free and rational creature that he is: all man's activity, whether feeling, thinking, or willing, depends more upon the power of the first cause, God, than upon man himself and his own power. As men, we are instruments in the hands of God, free instruments but, in the last analysis, instruments.

The exercise of the presence of God depends upon three truths of the natural order: God is in me; God sees me; God works in me.

God is present in things by His very substance, which, being immense, fills everything. He is present by His knowledge, which, as infinite, knows everything. He is present by His power, which moves every creature, God being the first and omnipotent cause of all. This threefold presence of God pertains to the natural order and is found in all creatures. It is found in all men, even those in the state of mortal sin.

But there is a new presence of God found only in the soul that has been supernaturalized. This presence is not only of the one God but of the one God who is three Persons. If we possess divine grace, there is present in us the Father who loves us as sons, the Son who loves us as brothers, and the Holy Spirit who showers us with gifts.

This presence of the triune God in the soul justified through grace is a great marvel. Neither man nor angel nor any other creature can enter by its own proper power into association with God in God's own intimate life. The intimate life of God consists in those mysterious relations that constitute the three Divine Persons. The Father, knowing Himself, begets the Word; and the Father and the Word, loving each other, give origin to the Holy Spirit. These relations cannot be externalized. Since all God's attributes pertain to the nature that is common to the three Divine Persons, everything that God does "outside" — *ad extra*, as the theologians say — He does not as triune but simply as one.

God causes the universe. But far from excluding any one of the three Persons, this act is common to all three. God knows all that exists. But this knowledge is not peculiar to the Father alone or the Son or the Holy Spirit; it is common to the three Persons. God governs the universe. But God's providence pertains to God as one, not as triune. All these associations of God with creatures, and consequently of creatures with God, are with God as one, not with God as triune.

But what is impossible to a creature is not impossible for God. And here is the ingenious way, if we may so speak, in which God in fact has overcome a difficulty and given us a share in His own divine life. The second Person of the Blessed Trinity, the Word, united Himself personally with a soul and with a body. In this way, one member of the human race, a representative of humanity, penetrated into the intimate life of God. The work of the Incarnation, since it is "outside" or *ad extra*, is common to the three Divine Persons. Nevertheless, the hypostatic union does not take place with either the Father or the Holy Spirit, but only with the Word. The humanity of Jesus Christ was the first created nature after the Fall to have special relations in a unique way not only with God as one but with God as triune. "The firstborn amongst many brethren," says St. Paul, of our Savior (Rom. 8:29).

Now by means of grace, the source of which is Jesus Christ, we are incorporated into Christ. Through His mediation, we, lowly creatures though we are, penetrate into the Holy of Holies that is the intimate life of God. It is natural that grace, which resides in Jesus Christ as in its fountainhead, should adapt itself to the special character of the second Person of the Blessed Trinity, who is Son par excellence. The grace that we receive is a grace of sonship; we are sons along with the Son. The Father is our Father, and the Holy Spirit, who is the Spirit of the Son and the Father, is also our Spirit. The Holy Spirit moves, governs, and sanctifies us, consummating our union with the Father and the Son.

Here, then, is a new wonder: not only is God in me, as Creator, Conserver, and Governor of the universe; He is also in me as tri-une, as three Persons, and has made my soul His lasting dwelling place. He does this not in a passing way but in a kind of definitive way. If I should lose God's presence, it will not be because God has first withdrawn His gifts but because I have voluntarily renounced them. Moreover, God is present not as a stranger—as He is present in the sinner—but as a beloved guest who comes to me in order that I may rejoice in His company and conversation. He comes to me in order that I may live, as St. John says, in communion with the Father, Son, and Holy Spirit. God is with me as Father, enveloping my soul in infinite tenderness. He is present as Word, illuminating me with a never-failing light, causing me to rejoice in the intimacy of brother and friend. He is in me as Holy Spirit, directing and sanctifying me with His gifts.

This, then, is the first truth of the supernatural order on which the exercise of the presence of God is founded: the Father, Son, and Holy Spirit are dwelling in me. I do not have to search them out in the heights of the heavens. I need only enter within myself; my soul, and even my body, is a temple in which dwell the "Three."

Perhaps this supernatural presence of God in the soul may appear too lofty for those just beginning the spiritual life. If beginners have not an exercise of the presence of God that supplies food for the imagination, the imagination will roam away into harmful distractions. But fortunately Jesus Christ is not only true God but also true man. He can be touched not only by our faith but also in a certain manner by our senses. Moreover, as we shall see later, it is impossible to reach the Divinity without passing through Jesus, the Mediator. The most sacred humanity of Jesus is the one road that can take us to the Divinity. The exercise of the presence of God becomes the exercise of the presence of Jesus.

What is the dogmatic foundation of this new presence? Jesus, as man—that is, in His sacred humanity—is not to be found really except in Heaven and in the consecrated host. One might suppose then that the presence of Jesus in us or near us is a pure figment of our imagination. Nevertheless, the following points must be kept in mind. First, whenever we pray before the tabernacle, the presence of Jesus is absolutely real. Jesus is very near us. Second, every time we receive Communion and so long as the sacred species remains, the presence of Jesus in our soul is absolutely real. Third, between Communions something of Jesus remains in us. Did not He Himself affirm, "He who eats My flesh, and drinks My blood, abides in Me and I in him"? (John 6:57). Deposit an exquisite perfume in an urn and the scent remains long after the liquid has disappeared. Now, when Jesus passes through our souls, He leaves them scented with His divine fragrance. Souls that have received Communion should spread everywhere the good odor of Christ.

What is it that Jesus leaves with us from one Communion to the other? First, He leaves sanctifying grace, which is increased. He leaves also the sacramental grace proper to the Eucharist. Grace is a life that Jesus as God and man communicates to us. It is the fruit of the sacrifice in which His most sacred humanity was immolated. It is the price of His blood, the fruit of His body, given over to death for our sakes.

A son invariably has about him something of his father, for he has received from his father nothing less than life itself. Now we have much of Jesus Christ in us, if we have received from Him the life of grace. Moreover, consider that although a father gives his son life, once he has given life, that life is independent of himself; a son can continue to live though his father die. The life of grace as we receive it from Jesus is different. The life of grace cannot continue even one moment in us without the constant and direct influence of Jesus Christ upon us. Jesus Christ exercises this vital influx on our souls not only as God but also as man. To be sure, there is something in us of Jesus.

What is this something of Jesus that is in our souls? Let us first of all relate it to the fact that Jesus sees us. He knows us not only with His divine knowledge but also with His human knowledge. It is common teaching, which cannot be denied without a grave sin of presumption, that even as man Jesus knows perfectly each and every human being that has ever existed in the past, that exists now, or that will exist in the future. His role of Redeemer and Sanctifier of the human race requires this. Jesus Himself tells us that He knows His sheep and that He calls each by its own proper name. He knows His own, not vaguely and confusedly but particularly. He knows every characteristic trait. His knowledge is integral, intimate, and complete.

What a consolation to realize that Jesus sees us and that His gaze follows us everywhere! His gaze is not a cold one. Still less is it severe or inquisitorial. Jesus' look is full of tenderness and love. It is the look that transformed Peter, converted Magdalene, and entangled the rich young man of whom we read in the Gospel.

Moreover, Jesus not only sees us but also loves us. He loves us as God; He loves us as man. His heart, as the Church exclaims in the preface of the Mass for the feast of the Sacred Heart, has never ceased to burn with love toward each and every soul — *flagrare numquam destitit.*[1] Spirits do not approach or move away according to material distances. They come near through understanding and especially through love. They move away through misunderstanding or indifference, and especially through hate. Two souls that know and love each other are united, even though separated by the immensity of the ocean or the vastness of the desert. If the heart of Jesus loves us, as it certainly does, and if we also love it, as our conscience bears witness that we do, then Jesus and ourselves, far from being separated by the immense distance between Heaven and earth, are intimately united by the indestructible bonds of love.

This "something" of Jesus that is in us is, in short, a vital inflow. Besides seeing and loving us, Jesus causes the life of grace to pulsate in our souls. He conserves and increases this life, and by means of His actual graces exerts an efficacious influence upon our whole spiritual activity. The dogma of the Mystical Body of Christ teaches us this. As the head exerts a vital and permanent influence over the whole organism, so Jesus Christ, head of His Mystical Body, exercises a vital, permanent, and absolutely essential influence on each and every one of His members. If there be any difference, it lies in the superiority of the reality over the symbol. The supernatural reality of the Mystical Body surpasses immensely the lowly realities of the natural order that symbolize it.

We see, now, the theological foundation of the presence of Jesus. Jesus not only as God but also as man sees us and loves us. He exercises a vital, constant, necessary, and efficacious influence on our whole supernatural life. For this reason, the rule that we have

---

[1] This wording is from the extraordinary form of the Roman Rite. —Ed.

just been explaining proposes not only that we exercise ourselves in the presence of God but also that we try to achieve the presence of Jesus. Our goal is to be no longer able to live alone, but only in intimate, constant, and delightful union with our Savior.

Rule 9

In order to avoid illusions, we need a sound, clear, and practical notion of holiness. Holiness consists in the faithful and constant fulfillment of our everyday duties.

Since all Christians are called to holiness, nothing is more important in the spiritual life than an adequate notion of what holiness is. This notion must be sound and clear, concrete and practical. One can hardly make intelligent progress toward a goal he has not quite located.

If our notion of holiness is to be sound, it should rest not on the more or less probable opinions of men but on the solid foundation of Sacred Scripture. The dogmatic teaching of the Church should be its support. To be clear, it should be expressed in a formula accessible to all. Moreover, it should be expressed in words that do not require philosophical and theological training to be understood. To be concrete, it must avoid vague abstractions and illusory idealism. To be practical, it should enable us to see what we must do in the concrete circumstances of everyday life in order to arrive at holiness. Let us look, then, for just such a concept of holiness: sound, clear, concrete, practical.

Only God is substantially and absolutely holy, the very essence of holiness. "*Tu solus sanctus*," the Church sings in the Gloria of the

Mass. "Thou alone art holy."[2] Man cannot be holy except accidentally or by participation. Man is holy in the measure in which he participates in God's holiness and unites himself with God. Now, as a creature, he is fundamentally and radically united to God by grace. Through grace, as St. Peter says, we are made "partakers of the divine nature" (2 Pet. 1:4). This participation is not simply moral, as nominalists and Protestants contend, consisting purely in the rectitude of the human will as imitating the divine will. It is a formal and physical participation, as the light of the atmosphere may be called a participation in the light of the sun. At the same time, it is an analogical participation, imitating in an accidental and imperfect way something that in God is perfect and substantial.

Now, a thing cannot become one with fire and not burn, or one with light and not be illuminated. In the same way, if God is holiness itself, it is impossible to participate in His nature without participating in His holiness. Therefore, as our participation in the divine nature, grace radically sanctifies; this is why it is called sanctifying grace. As soon as one is in the state of grace, he possesses at least an initial holiness. In the measure in which grace develops, he progresses in holiness. To the full development of grace in the present life, there corresponds the highest degree of sanctity for this particular individual. Holiness in man is not something absolute, but relative. It does not come all in one piece, nor is it achieved all at once. It is progressive and develops little by little as a seed develops into a tree. We receive the seed of holiness the day of our Baptism; if we cultivate it, it will someday come to full maturity.

Radically and fundamentally united to God by grace, we are formally and ultimately united to Him by charity. Grace makes us

---

[2]   This wording is from the extraordinary form of the Roman Rite.
    —Ed.

godlike in the order of being and charity in the order of activity, just as in the natural order the soul makes us to be men, and the faculties of the soul, intellect and will, enable us to act as men. He is most holy who possesses the most charity. There is one charity in Heaven and on earth; if charity unites us to God there, it does so here on earth also. Charity makes us like God and sanctifies us precisely because it unites us to God. Holiness, formally considered, consists in charity.

But between the charity we have at justification and the charity of the saints, there are innumerable degrees. And to these degrees there correspond so many steps in the steep climb up the road to holiness. The charity that makes us truly saints is not incipient charity but perfect, fervent, active charity. In order to have the perfect charity of the saints, we must get rid of all obstacles to charity by exercising the moral virtues, and we must exercise the theological virtues also. Faith and confidence in God are necessary, since we cannot love what we do not know and desire. Moreover, the virtues cannot be exercised in all their perfection without the predominating exercise of the gifts of the Holy Spirit. To arrive at integral holiness, we must, then, possess all the moral and theological virtues in their perfection; and the gifts of the Holy Spirit must be operative in a predominating way. Holiness radically consists in sanctifying grace; formally, in charity; integrally, in the perfected virtues and the gifts.

Perhaps I find such a complex and speculative notion of holiness disheartening. I find myself perplexed, undecided, confused. When will I succeed in acquiring all the virtues? Where should I begin? How are the gifts exercised?

Rules for the Spiritual Life

Actually, for practical purposes, the notion of sanctity can be considerably simplified. Concretely and practically, I can ask, what ought I to do, in a practical way, to arrive at holiness? Not only will the canonical or ecclesiastical notion of holiness help us answer this question, but the procedure followed by the Church in the process of the beatification and canonization of saints will shed full light on it. Before placing a soul on the altar, for veneration by the faithful, the Church opens a most difficult and delicate process, the process of beatification. The chief and most laborious part of this process consists in proving that the four moral virtues and three theological virtues have been exercised to a heroic degree. When this has been established, a person acquires the title "Venerable."

In earlier times, the virtues were taken up one by one. Relevant facts were brought forth from the life of the servant of God to manifest each virtue. The task was laborious and difficult and often ended in failure.

At the present time, the method of procedure has been simplified. It now consists in demonstrating that the person in question fulfilled his or her everyday tasks with perfection and constancy, in this way conforming fully with the divine will. Perfect conformity of the human will with the divine will—it is in this that holiness consists. Benedict XV was the first to open this way. In 1916, at the proclamation of the heroic virtue of the young Franciscan John Baptiste de Bourgogne, for the first time in a canonical process heroic virtue was said to consist simply in the faithful and constant fulfillment of one's duties and obligations.

In the decree concerning the heroic virtue of Ven. Antonio Cianelli, in 1920, this same doctrine was expounded with more precision. Sanctity was declared to consist properly in the complete conformity of the human will with the divine will; this conformity was said to be manifested in the constant and exact fulfillment of the duties proper to one's state. Such a manner of living, persevered in unswervingly over a long period of time, is beyond the power of human nature left to itself. Left to himself, man is a plaything of the ups and downs of life, especially because of the inconstancy of his passions. The exact and faithful fulfillment of duty supposes the exclusion of all deliberate imperfection; otherwise there would be lacking the generosity that heroism requires.

But it was above all Pius XI who taught this doctrine magisterially when he proclaimed the virtues of the relatively little-known Bl. Benildo, Brother of the Christian Schools. The Holy Father called Bl. Benildo "a humble servant of God, whose life was all modesty and silence, quite common and ordinary."

"But how uncommon and extraordinary," the Holy Father continued, as quoted in *L'Osservatore Romano*,

> is such a life lived every day! This daily duty which is always being reborn and which is every day the same, which consists always in the same occupations, which carries with it the same weaknesses and the same miseries! It has been called the terrible everyday duty.
>
> What efforts are needed to defend oneself against this terrible, this crushing, this monotonous, this suffocating everyday duty. By no means common virtue is required to fulfill one's daily duty with uncommon exactitude. Or better, there is required an extraordinary virtue not to act with the so common and daily and frequent carelessness, negligence, and superficiality ... but to act, on the contrary, with attention, piety, and inner fervor of spirit.
>
> The Holy Church has never manifested herself a more equitable and wiser teacher of holiness than when raising up these humble lights, so frequently ignored even by those

who had the good fortune to see them shining right before their eyes.

Extraordinary things, great events, fine enterprises arouse and awaken great enthusiasm as soon as they are mentioned. The common and the ordinary quite to the contrary. That which presents nothing outstanding and no splendor whatsoever, which is in no way attractive or fascinating, is relegated to the merely everyday.

And nevertheless it is this which makes up the life of the great majority of people. Ordinary life is made up of common things and everyday events. How many times in life do extraordinary things present themselves? Very rarely. And how unfortunate this is for us if holiness must be reserved only for extraordinary circumstances! What then would be the lot of the greater part of men? For, we repeat, the call to sanctity comes to all without distinction.

The Holy Father is here directing his teaching to the whole world. There remains, therefore, no doubt that heroic sanctity, the sanctity the Church glorifies on her altars and presents to all the faithful as a model to be imitated, consists in the constant and faithful fulfillment of the "terrible everyday duty."

This everyday duty includes everything: the commandments of God, the precepts of the Church, professional duties, and the duties of one's state. It applies equally well in every walk of life: to priests, religious, parents, children, doctors, lawyers, businessmen, employers, laborers, servants. It extends beyond duty in the strict sense to include every inspiration of grace. It applies to every occasion of doing good that presents itself and to every form of the apostolate within our reach.

Rule 9

Sure of this truth upon the authority of the Supreme Pontiff, we can look for the reasons that justify it. How does the constant and faithful fulfillment of the "terrible everyday duty" suppose heroic sanctity?

We have already seen that holiness essentially consists in charity; not in an idle and remiss charity but one that is active and fervent. Now our Lord has taught us in what the perfection of charity itself consists: "Not everyone who says to me 'Lord, Lord,' shall enter the kingdom of heaven; but he who does the will of my Father in heaven shall enter the kingdom of heaven" (Matt. 7:21). And St. Paul tells us that not those who hear the law are just (that is, holy before God), but those who fulfill it; they are holy (Rom. 2:13). On the night before He died, Jesus affirmed again: "He who has my commandments and keeps them [that is, he who carries out my will], he it is who loves me." "If any one love me, he will keep my word" (John 14:21; 14:23). In the Lord's Prayer, He taught us that His Father is glorified and that His reign, or holiness, is established among men when His will is fulfilled on earth as it is in Heaven. Holiness, then, must consist in the union of our will with the will of God. The more perfect the conformity of our will with God's, so much the greater is our holiness. Now, in a practical and concrete way, the will of God is manifested to us in every moment of our lives by means of the "terrible everyday duty." The duty of everyday is nothing else but the concrete manifestation of the divine will, according to the circumstances and state of life of each one of us.

But why call it the "terrible" everyday duty? Far from exceeding our natural powers assisted by ordinary grace, to fulfill it on this day and at this hour is of itself admittedly easy. But think what it means to fulfill our duty every day of our life, in youth, maturity, and old age; in the full vigor of our powers and in their decay; in the enthusiasm of beginning an undertaking and in the disillusionment that time brings with it; in health and in sickness; in success and in failure; in prosperity and humiliation; in periods of sensible fervor and supernatural consolation as also in periods of dryness and desolation; in a word, across all the vicissitudes of life! Think what it means to fulfill this everyday duty not only with a constancy that cannot be discouraged but with a fidelity and effort that exclude every remiss act and every voluntary imperfection.

Is it not evident that such an achievement exceeds the forces of nature, even assisted by ordinary grace? Such an achievement requires a perfection of charity and of the other virtues inconceivable without an extraordinary fullness of grace. For such an accomplishment, grace must have made a man godlike in his being, and the activity of the gifts of the Holy Spirit must have made him godlike in his operations. Governed and directed by the Holy Spirit in his every action, he has arrived at heroic sanctity, or sanctity in all its fullness. The duty is called "terrible," because it requires a heroism and fortitude greater than that of a martyr. Such a manner of living is attained only in the ultimate period of life and is a direct prelude to the consummation of eternity.

The mountain peak of heroic sanctity is lofty and the road leading upward to it long. But the road is open before us and the first steps along it easily within our reach. We have simply to carry out our daily duties. The road is even easier if we begin each day as if it were the only one. If we carry out each daily duty faithfully, our fidelity and constancy will grow almost without our realizing it. Through the years, we cannot but make great progress. But we must guard as a great treasure this truth that does not admit of illusions, and that embraces a notion of holiness at once sound, clear, concrete, and practical: holiness consists in the faithful and constant fulfillment of "the terrible everyday duty."

Rule 10

It is of capital importance that we learn to love the sacred humanity of Jesus, the cross, the Holy Eucharist, the Sacred Heart of Jesus, the Blessed Virgin Mary, and the Holy Spirit.

This rule alone comprises a whole program of the spiritual life. It expounds the characteristic notes of that school of spirituality known as "the spirituality of the cross," and at the same time firmly roots the whole spiritual life in dogma. There is only one road along which we can arrive at union with the divinity, and that road is the humanity of Jesus Christ, the one Mediator between God and men, the one Redeemer and Savior of the world. Our goal, perfection, consists in charity. Charity is the image of the Holy Spirit, but we reach the Holy Spirit only through the humanity of Jesus. Mary, the co-redemptrix and the mediatrix of all graces, is the means by which we go to the humanity of Jesus. "To Jesus through Mary."

In order to attract hearts and win their love, there have been three great manifestations of devotion to the humanity of Jesus: the cross, the Eucharist, and the Sacred Heart. The cross was the devotion of early Christianity. The Eucharist, the devotion of the Middle Ages, has continued developing right into our own time. The Sacred Heart, the devotion of recent times, stands as the supreme revelation of Christ.

These three aspects, these three devotions, would seem to be really but the revelation, each time more intimate, of the sacrifice of Christ, that sacrifice that is the cipher, key, and center of His whole life, mission, and holiness. Jesus Christ came into the world to sacrifice Himself. Through His sacrifice, He would redeem and sanctify souls and glorify His Father. The cross is the symbol of the external sacrifice of Christ. The Eucharist is His unbloody sacrifice, perpetuated through the centuries. The Sacred Heart, expressing His interior sacrifice and His internal sorrows, is, in the words of Msgr. Gay, "the passion of His heart and the heart of His passion."

The whole of the sacrifice of Jesus is a most clear revelation and most eloquent demonstration of His love for men. No one loves so much as he who gives his life for those he loves: "Greater love than this no one has, that one lay down his life for his friends" (John 15:13). The whole life of Christ can be summed up in two words, love and sorrow, or as St. Paul says: *In caritate et patientia Christi* — in the love and suffering of Christ (2 Thess. 3:5).

Dogmatic and Historical Aspects of This Rule

The divine wisdom, which tolerates evil only in order to draw from it greater good, has willed to permit that from the days of the Church's birth to the end of time, heresies should constantly arise against various teachings of the Faith. And from this great evil of heresy, God draws a greater good. With the combating of heresies and the defending of revealed truths, dogma itself has been progressively clarified and made more precise. This clarification has proceeded particularly from the writings of the Holy Fathers, the Doctors of the Church, and the sacred writers, and above all from the orientations and dogmatic definitions of the Holy See.

As might have been expected, the first heresy to appear in the Church was the denial of the divinity of Jesus Christ. Jesus had been seen by all as a man; nobody was able to put the reality of His sacred humanity in doubt. But He had affirmed that He was

God as well. Now a God who would die crucified and conquered by His enemies could not appear less than a contradiction. From the beginning of the Christian era, Cerinthians, Essenes, Ebionites, Gnostics, and Theodosians denied the divinity of Jesus, just as did, later on, the Arians and the Cathari, and in more recent times the Free Thinkers and Modernists. These groups represent the Rationalists of all times.

The apostle John wrote his incomparable Gospel to demonstrate the divinity of Jesus Christ. On terminating his Gospel, he himself says, "But these are written that you may believe that Jesus is the Christ, the Son of God" (John 20:31). The Synoptics, Matthew, Mark, and Luke, speak in a special way of Christ as man. John, represented by the eagle, spreads his wings and rises up to the divinity of Christ from the very beginning of his Gospel: "In the beginning was the Word, and the Word was with God; and the Word was God" (John 1:1).

In the fourth century, there appeared the great heresy of Arianism, which, if it had come later, would have produced in the Church a break as definitive as that produced by Protestantism. Arianism affirmed that Jesus Christ was an exceptional man, of a superior dignity to all other creatures, through whom all of them were created. But Jesus Christ was not God, consubstantial with the Father. He was only the adopted Son of God. Arianism won so many adherents and spread itself so successfully under the patronage of the emperors that, as St. Jerome put it, "The whole world groaned, and was amazed to see itself Arian."

The Church was intent in this world controversy on affirming the divinity of Jesus Christ. The humanity of Jesus, universally acknowledged, naturally received less attention. Since the spiritual life shares the lot of dogma, the emphasis on the divinity of Christ inevitably had repercussions in spirituality. The iconography or image-making of these early centuries reflects the devotion, and the devotion reflects the dogmatic stress on our Lord's divinity. Nobody dared represent the crucified Christ with the tragic and bloody realism with which we are accustomed to contemplate Him today. True, Jesus was depicted on the Cross. His Cross, however, was not a gibbet but a throne. Jesus was not depicted naked and bloody but clothed in priestly or royal vesture. He was crowned not with thorns but with an imperial diadem. He was represented not with the tortured muscular contractions of a man executed for a crime but with a serene and majestic air of triumph. In a word, the triumph of the Cross was represented, not its shame. From His Cross, Christ reigned over the world.

The devotion to the Infant Jesus also reflects the stress on our Savior's divinity. The Church of the first centuries celebrated the feast of the Nativity as devoutly as we do. But this feast then commemorated rather what we commemorate in the Epiphany. The royalty of Jesus stood out manifested to the world. More importance was given to the God who received the gold and the incense than to the man who received the myrrh.

The devotion to the Holy Eucharist is another example. In the first centuries of Christianity, the Eucharist was kept hidden in the catacombs, a great secret among Christians. When the peace of Constantine came, Christians considered the Eucharist especially in its sacrificial aspect. The Eucharist was not reserved except for the purpose of giving Viaticum to the sick. As a result, the most sacred place in the church was not the tabernacle, which did not exist, but the altar. When the Holy Eucharist was reserved, it was kept concealed, sometimes in a dove suspended over the altar, sometimes in a kind of little tower placed with its back next to a column of the sanctuary, or sometimes in a little closet opening into the wall behind the altar or even in the sacristy. Because the presence of the Blessed Sacrament was difficult to recognize, the faithful venerated preferably the altar, solemnly consecrated by the bishop; there the precious relics of the martyrs were kept, and there each day the divine mysteries were celebrated.

In the Middle Ages, the controversies about the divinity of Christ subsided. This dogma having been solidly secured, a healthy reaction appeared in favor of the humanity of our Lord. "The great novelty and incomparable religious merit of the Middle Ages," asserts Rousselot, "is the understanding and love, or better, the passionate love, of the humanity of Christ. The incarnate Word, the man Christ Jesus, not only is the model whom it is necessary to imitate, the guide whom it is necessary to follow, the uncreated light who illuminates the interior of the soul; He is also the friend, the spouse." He is the mystical spouse of the soul who lives with it in "stupendous familiarity" (*familiaritas stupenda nimis*), as the author of the *Imitation* says.

Devotion to the humanity of Christ unquestionably belongs to every age of the Church. How many admirable pages could be cited from St. John, St. Paul, St. Ignatius of Antioch, and St. Augustine, to mention a few! But in the Middle Ages there developed in this devotion a tenderness so simple, intimate, ardent, that it must be considered as something new.

St. Bernard of Clairvaux and St. Francis of Assisi are among the principal initiators of this movement. The sermons of St. Bernard form a kind of mystical biography of the Savior, in which their author finds delight in considering especially the infancy and the Passion. "Upon seeing the Child in Bethlehem and the Man of

Sorrows," says Vernet, "he becomes tender, he is filled with confusion, he weeps and finds himself ready for whatever generosity the imitation of Christ demands, for every heroism of love."

One passage from St. Bernard will manifest his tender, personal love for the Savior.

> I hail You, Jesus my beloved. I desire to place myself upon Your Cross. You know the reason why. Give Yourself to me. From the height of Your Cross, my beloved, look down upon me. Draw me wholly to Yourself. Once again say to me, "I pardon you!" See how, all on fire and enraptured by Your love, I embrace You. I press You to my heart. Support me. Do not say anything. Let not my boldness displease You.

St. Francis of Assisi was an equally passionate lover of Jesus. What was the road taken by St. Francis when he turned to God, to be united to Him in the loftiest sanctity? First of all, God made use of his natural temperament. From the time of Francis's youth, two great qualities are evident: an extreme generosity and an exquisite sensibility. His generosity led him to give everything away, until he reached the point of extravagance and provoked the anger of his father. His sensibility caused misery and suffering to move him to tears. Francis was at first charitable to the poor more through temperament than through virtue. Their misery moved him and he showered them prodigally with gifts. But one day God gave him a great light, and he discerned in the poor none other than Jesus Christ Himself. Upon his discovery of his Lord and God in the persons of the poor, his exquisite sensibility was profoundly moved. His generosity prompted him to give not his gifts but himself in complete and total oblation.

Francis of Assisi fell in love with Christ, contemplating Him above all in three mysteries of His life: Bethlehem, Calvary, and the Eucharist. In his personal appreciation of these mysteries, we can say that Francis of Assisi was truly original, quite independent of St. Bernard, whom perhaps he had never read. The feast of the Nativity, translated into the beautiful crib representations of Bethlehem, was an invention of the exquisite sensibility and incomparable tenderness of St. Francis. With what tenderness he took into his arms and pressed to his breast the image of the Infant Savior! Those hands that later on were to be torn by the stigmata cradled the image of the Christ Child with childlike simplicity and candor. The feast of the Nativity in that moment acquired the special mark of simplicity and childlike joy that causes us today to become children again in contemplating the immortal Infant of Bethlehem. Christian art began to represent not only the Child-God adored by the Magi but also, and above all, the poor little Child of Bethlehem wrapped in swaddling clothes and lying in a manger.

Francis of Assisi was also the forerunner of what has been called "the passion for the Passion of the Savior." In order to love Jesus Crucified, he himself was mystically crucified while still living, and he merited the grace of bearing in his afflicted body the five wounds of the Savior.

Finally, he was the pioneer in that great eucharistic movement that began in the thirteenth century, and that has continued to grow until reaching that splendid high noon that lights up the Catholic devotion of today. Francis of Assisi loved the Eucharist because, as he said, "it is the one sensible manifestation that we still have of the Son of God."

Homocentrism and Theocentrism

We have just seen how the devotion of the first centuries of Christianity especially emphasized Jesus Christ as God while that of the

Middle Ages especially emphasized Jesus Christ as man. In what has been called the "French school" of devotion of the seventeenth century, these two aspects achieved an admirable synthesis. The spirituality of this school has for its center Jesus Christ, the incarnate Word. But it does not consider Him either precisely as God or precisely as man, but in all His fullness and integrity—that is, as God-Man. It studies each one of the mysteries of the mortal life of Jesus Christ, but not so much in each historical act that by its nature passes, as in the interior disposition the incarnate Word had in these mysteries. Such a disposition does not pass but endures as a "state."

Although this spirituality is said to be of the French school, it has had great influence in the whole Church, its principal representatives being founders of religious families destined for the education and formation of the clergy in the Church's seminaries. Among its leaders are Cardinal Berulle, founder of the Oratory of Jesus; Fr. Olier, founder of the Sulpicians; St. Vincent de Paul, founder of the Vincentians; St. John Eudes, founder of the Eudists; and writers of importance such as Condren, Saint-Jure, and Msgr. Gay.

To understand this movement better, we must recall that there have always been in the Church two currents, two systems or schools of spirituality: homocentrism and theocentrism. Perfectly orthodox, both schools end up by uniting man with God. But they differ in the road they follow and the means they employ, or perhaps better, in their point of view.

Homocentrism, dominant in the centuries preceding the seventeenth, concerned itself directly with the task of perfecting man. It began by studying him. It can be broadly expressed in that great maxim that sums up all of Greek philosophy and was written in letters of gold in the temple of Delphi, "Know thyself."

In this spirituality, the examination of conscience naturally receives great stress. Through the examination of conscience, a man enters into himself in order to study and know himself. He must know his defects and correct them; he must know his good qualities and foster them. Hence the prominence of the particular examen, by means of which a person proceeds to correct defect after defect or to inculcate virtue after virtue. Sometimes each defect or virtue is broken down into its numerous parts, and a person works to improve himself almost "piece by piece."

Prayer, common to all spirituality, takes on a special character in homocentrism. It is considered as necessarily oriented toward the reform of life, the correcting of defects and the practice of virtues. Prayer must always culminate in a specific, practical resolution. This is prayer in its utilitarian aspect. Likewise, the way to grow in some particular virtue in this school is to consider the virtue in itself, its necessity, its advantages, its beauty, so that one will be moved to practice it. A like procedure applies to vices and defects. A person reflects on their ugliness, the disadvantages that they carry with them, and so on, in order that he may be moved to correct himself.

How many well-known Christian expressions have their inspirations in homocentrism! For example, the famous saying of St. Augustine: "O Lord, Thou hast made us for Thyself, and our heart is restless until it rest in Thee." St. Augustine concerns himself above all with the interior state of his soul and with the restlessness that afflicts it. Sad experience teaches him that his restless soul can find rest only in God. He comes therefore to this conclusion: God has made us for Himself. All of this he then expresses in an order the inverse of that in which he discovered it. Thomas à Kempis

manifests himself a homocentrist when he gives assurance that
God is our supreme and final end "if we truly desire to be happy"
(*si vere desideras esse beatus*).

Theocentrism begins to predominate precisely with the French
school of which we were speaking earlier. It stresses the truth that
our perfection is above all a life, a life of which the source is Jesus
Christ. The most efficacious means to attain perfection is to unite
ourselves to that life. We are to adhere to Jesus Christ, assimilate
His states to ourselves, make His dispositions ours, commune
with His mysteries. Little by little, the life of Christ will come to
supplant, or, perhaps better, to transform our human lives, so that
it is no longer we who live but Christ who lives in us.

Resting upon this principle, theocentrism considers everything
from a divine vantage point. In this school, too, man tries to know
himself. But he tries to know himself in comparison with God and
by the light of contrasts, as night is known by contemplating the
clear brightness of day. He tries to correct his defects and practice
the virtues; however, he considers virtues not precisely in themselves but rather as incarnated in Jesus Christ. By contemplating
the humble Jesus and joining himself to the humility of Jesus, he
will hate pride more and practice humility with greater energy.

Just as it is impossible to carry perfume on one's person without becoming saturated by its fragrance, just as we cannot expose
ourselves to the sun without having its rays warm us, so we cannot
put ourselves into contact with the virtues of Christ and not become impregnated by those virtues. If there are bodies that have a
mysterious power to cure and the presence of which alone destroys
harmful germs, how much more must Jesus Christ have power to
purify and sanctify our souls. During His mortal life there went

forth from Him a power capable of healing all (see Luke 6:19); and now there goes forth from His glorified body and His most holy soul a power that purifies us of all our stains and impregnates us with all His virtues.

Nor should anyone suppose that this system dispenses us from the personal effort of correcting our defects and practicing the virtues. It does not dispense us from doing these things; but it does facilitate our doing them. It gives more importance to the efficacy of grace than to our personal efforts, but it does not deny the necessity of either the one or the other.

In theocentrism, prayer has as its end to adore and praise God, and all prayer is directed toward establishing this divine contact. Following its union with God, the soul rests in God, without seeking expressly anything more. This prayer is not ordered directly to the correction of defects. But is it not clear that the soul will come forth from this association with God more resolved to renounce itself, more determined upon charity toward others, more intent on all the various virtues even if it has not expressly formulated concrete resolutions?

Spirituality of the Cross

The spirituality of the cross has a very close connection with the spirituality of the French school of the seventeenth century. It is theocentric, or, perhaps better, Christocentric. However, it is not a simple copy, a superfluous reproduction of the spirituality of the French school. Nor is it exactly an adaptation of that spirituality to our own environment and our own time. It has its own originality and its own proper characteristics that are admirably summed up in the rule upon which we are commenting. Its basic principle is a passionate love for the humanity of Jesus Christ. In this respect, it is related to medieval spirituality. This spirituality considers in a special way three manifestations of devotion to the humanity of Jesus, which mark, at the same time, the three great stages through which this devotion has evolved. First, the cross symbolizes the sufferings of Jesus in His Passion. The Eucharist is the means by which the humanity of Jesus, in addition to being in Heaven, is also found in our midst, exposed for our adoration in the monstrance, immolated on our altars, and given to us as food in Holy Communion. Finally, the Sacred Heart is the symbol of the human-divine love with which Jesus has loved us, and of the interior sorrows that lasted throughout His mortal life and mysteriously continue in the Holy Eucharist. Unquestionably, Jesus is in the Holy Eucharist in a state of glory, incompatible with the physical or moral suffering proper to passible beings. Nevertheless, the revelations of St. Margaret Mary, and even more significantly the encyclical *Miserentissimus Redemptor*, make us aware of the mystical sorrows of the heart of Jesus, begging of us our consolation and compassion. Devotion to the humanity of Jesus in the spirituality of the cross aims to unite us with that sacred humanity, incorporate us into it, until a perfect assimilation is reached.

The first stage consists in participating in the Passion of Christ by means of mortification, according to the words of St. Peter: "In so far as you are partakers of the sufferings of Christ" (1 Pet. 4:13). This mortification purifies our souls, disposing them for the second stage.

The second stage is eucharistic. We have already noted that all the mysteries of Christ have Christ's sacrifice as the center around which they converge, the key that explains them, and the symbol that expresses them. Now the sacrifice of Christ, consummated on the Cross and perpetuated in the Eucharist, finds its consummation on earth in the hearts of the faithful and in Heaven on that "sublime altar" of which the liturgy speaks in the Canon of the Mass. Purified through its communication with the Passion of Christ and by means of true Christian mortification, the soul is transformed, so to speak, into a living altar where the incarnate Word continues His immolation and perpetuates His sacrifice. In this sacrifice the soul is not a simple spectator; it is an altar, a priest that offers, and a victim offered.

The soul makes constant offering to the Word and is offered with Him on the altar of its heart for the glory of the Father and the sanctification of souls. This offering is something more than an act that is repeated; it is a "state" or a habitual disposition.

When the soul has been assimilated and transformed into the incarnate Word, participating intimately in that act that is most fundamental and essential to Him, that is, in His sacrifice, it enters into the intimate sanctuary of the divine heart. It receives a special understanding of Christ's interior sorrows and, even more important, it receives the grace to participate in them in some way. This is the third stage, the stage of spiritual fecundity. The sacrifice of Christ saved the world; and most central in the sacrifice of Christ is His interior suffering. When the soul participates in these sorrows, it continues in a certain way the redemptive work of Christ on earth.

It is a teaching of faith that no creature, however perfect, can enter into relations through its own proper powers with each one of the Divine Persons. Man can place himself in relation with God; but with God as one, not with God as triune; with God the author of nature, not with God the author of grace.

Reason also tells us this. Let us suppose that man had not been elevated to the supernatural order; that, consequently, he did not have the light of faith nor the teachings of revelation, but only the natural light of reason. Sacred Scripture teaches us that in this case man could still rise through creatures to knowledge of his Creator (see Rom. 1:20). Nobody of sound mind can in fact contemplate the universe with its most wise laws, its admirable order, and its unequaled beauty without concluding that someone has created it. And He who created the universe must be superior to it, more perfect, more beautiful than it is. Reasoning in this way, even pagans have arrived at a knowledge of God as author of the universe.

But all the attributes of God that put Him in relation with His creatures pertain to the divine nature, and consequently to God as one, not to God as triune: His omnipotence, for example, by which He created us; His providence, by which He governs us; His goodness, by which He heaps benefits upon us; His wisdom, by which He orders all that He has made. When we study creatures, we find in them a kind of reflection of these same attributes. From creation we infer the omnipotence of God; from the order in the universe, the divine wisdom; from the goodness and beauty of the universe, the goodness and beauty of God.

Now, the divine attributes pertain to the divine nature; they are not proper to one Person but common to all three. The Father is omnipotent, as are the Son and the Holy Spirit. The Father is wise, just as are the other two Divine Persons. The divine immensity, eternity, and other attributes are possessed by all three Persons. In the natural order we know God only through His attributes, manifested to us through creatures; and these pertain not to God as triune but to God as one. Consequently, in the natural order we can enter into relations with God only according to the unity of His nature and not according to the Trinity of Persons. God does not place Himself in relation with His creatures except by means of His attributes; consequently, not as God who is triune but as God who is one. The Holy Trinity, then, lives in a light inaccessible to man. The intimate life of God—the relations of the three Divine Persons among themselves—is a cloistered sanctuary as far as every creature is concerned. It is like the "Holy of Holies" of the Temple in Jerusalem, into which nobody could enter except the high priest and he only once a year.

But what was impossible to man's power was not impossible to God. Between the abyss in which man lay and the inaccessible light in which God dwelt, God stretched a gigantic bridge. God established a supreme mediator. "And the Word was made flesh, and dwelt among us" (John 1:14). The second Person of the Holy Trinity came down from His royal throne and united Himself in personal union to a human nature like ours. And this humanity was the first creature to enter into contact, into intimate relations, with each one of the three Divine Persons. From the moment in which the Word assumed it, that humanity became the human nature of the second Person of the Blessed Trinity. Christ in His sacred humanity, then, is the natural Son of God and can truly regard the divine Father as His Father and the Holy Spirit as His Spirit. In His sacred humanity He is the incarnate Word Himself.

Now this mystery of the Incarnation has a kind of prolongation in all creatures and in all the souls of the just. In another ineffable mystery, Jesus Christ unites us to His humanity, incorporates us into it. United to Him, incorporated into Him, we are His members and form one organic, vital unity with Christ our head. As a kind of prolongation of His most sacred humanity, we enter, united with it, into intimate relations with each one of the three Divine Persons. As the Son makes us partakers of His Sonship, we can legitimately call the Father of our Lord Jesus Christ "Our Father." The Spirit of the Father and the Son is also our Spirit, He who directs, moves, and governs us.

How is this incorporation carried out? How could Jesus graft us onto Himself in this way, so that we form a kind of prolongation of His most sacred humanity? The answer is grace. Here we meet with another new mystery, the mystery of our justification. Jesus Christ is constituted by God the source of grace for us. Or better, there is only one grace; it is the very divine life and has its source in God. To adapt it to our smallness, God has caused it to pass through the humanity of Jesus Christ. Through the humanity of Jesus Christ, it is poured into the souls of the just, as life-giving blood is distributed through the heart to the whole body.

Precisely because it comes to us from the Son, grace is marked with the characteristics of *filiation* or sonship. It makes us sons with the Son, causes us to receive the Spirit of adoption, and enables us to exclaim, "Abba, Father" (Rom. 8:15). Jesus Christ is the firstborn among many brethren, the great Mediator and High Priest. Through Him, the soul enters into relations not only with God as one but with God as triune. And these intimate relations with each one of the three Divine Persons constitute one of the fundamental characteristics of Catholic spirituality, including the spirituality of the cross.

The devotion that the majority of the faithful generally have toward the Holy Trinity unfortunately is not the devotion of which we have been speaking but rather devotion to divine providence. Moreover, as many practice this devotion, it is not without a certain self-interest, for it amounts to seeking the fundamental necessities of food, clothing, and shelter. Is not that person rare, even among the devout, who has a devotion to each of the three Divine Persons, particularizing his relations with each?

The life of Jesus Christ and our lives are in the supernatural order one and the same. Our parents give us life in the order of nature.

But after they have given it to us, we continue to live independently of them. In a much more perfect way, we have life from Jesus Christ, for not only do we get it from Him originally but we continue to receive it constantly. We cannot live in the supernatural order independently of Jesus Christ. He must exert a vital influence upon us at every moment. In all truth, we live the very life of Christ.

We are not united to Him only through a moral union. The members of a state form one moral body animated by what may be called "the soul of the nation"; when the country is in danger, all individuals, whatever their party or ideas, unite as one man with one heart for its defense. Now union with Christ by grace is a much closer union than this. Perhaps it could be called a physical union if it were not in the supernatural order. At any rate, it is unquestionably a *vital* union. In Christ and ourselves there throbs but one life. Christ does not have one life and we another; there is one life for both.

St. Paul offers the comparison with the vital union that is to be found among the different organs of the body. An organism is formed of various organs: eyes, ears, digestive and circulatory apparatus, the nervous system, and so on. But among all these organs there is a perfect unity, because the life that animates the eyes is the same as the life that animates the ears, the tongue, the muscles. In spite of the different functions of each organ, all have the same life. In the same way, but with a higher perfection, we are united with Jesus in one life.

St. Jerome says that all the grace found in Jesus Christ is found also in the Blessed Virgin, although in a different way. Grace is found in Jesus Christ as in our Redeemer and Sanctifier par excellence: it is in the Blessed Virgin as in our co-redemptrix and mediatrix. This is why we affirm, in contrast to Protestants, that the Blessed Virgin has an indispensable and necessary role in the actual economy of man's sanctification and salvation. In God's actual plan it is not possible to prescind from her, any more than it is possible to prescind from Jesus Christ. If Jesus Christ is our life, the Blessed Virgin is truly our Mother, because she has given us Jesus Christ. Our relations with the incarnate Word necessarily include the Blessed Virgin; Jesus Christ does not come to us except through her, nor does grace, the life of our souls, reach us except in passing through Mary. All men ought to have a special devotion to the mystery of the Immaculate Conception, in order to admire and venerate in this mystery the fullness of grace that God poured into Mary. In both the Gospel and the Offertory of the Mass of the Immaculate Conception, the Church repeats the angelic salutation: *"Ave Maria, gratia plena —* Hail Mary, full of grace."[3] Mary received grace in its fullness in order from that fullness to pass on grace to us.

A second consequence is that everything that belongs to Jesus Christ, as well as everything that belongs to the Blessed Virgin, is in some way ours. St. Paul tells us to "put on the Lord Jesus Christ" (Rom. 13:14). In order to appear to be his father's firstborn and so receive the blessing reserved for the firstborn, Jacob clothed himself with the perfumed vesture of the firstborn. And Jacob received the blessing (see Gen. 27:1-29). When we come to present ourselves to our heavenly Father, we ought to clothe ourselves with Jesus Christ so that our heavenly Father may not see our miseries but may see His Son, the Son of His eternal good pleasure, and through Him look upon us with the same good pleasure with which He looks upon His Son, thereby pardoning us our sins: "Look on the face of thy Christ" (Ps. 83:10).

---

[3] As given in the extraordinary form of the Roman Rite. — Ed.

The great secret of sanctity does not lie precisely in knowing our-selves, endlessly analyzing our actions, trying to discern our intention on some particular occasion. To know ourselves is important, but it is not everything. No, we must clothe ourselves with Jesus Christ, as the apostle tells us, make all that belongs to Christ ours, because in a certain way it is ours. The virtues of Jesus Christ are meant to be our virtues, His humility, our humility. We are to unite ourselves to Him so as to participate in the meekness of His divine heart. His charity is to be our charity, His prayer, our prayer, and His sacrifices, or better, sacrifice, is meant to be our sacrifice. Rather than for us to pray, Jesus Christ ought to be praying in us. Rather than for us to offer our little sacrifices, Jesus Christ ought to be sacrificing Himself in us. As we offer our poor sacrifices along with His great one, our sacrifices should become one with His. On the altar of our hearts, we ought to unite ourselves to that constant oblation that the divine Word makes of His sacrifice and ours, to constitute what has been called the "chain of love, the offering of the Word."

St. Paul tells us not only to put on Jesus Christ but to share His every disposition. "Have this mind in you which was also in Christ Jesus" (Phil. 2:5). Christ's outlook must become ours. When we pray, we ought to consider, "How would Jesus Christ pray?" In our dealings with others, we ought to ask, "What would Jesus Christ do here?" We should enter into Jesus' way of looking at things, into the purity of His intentions, into the dispositions of His adorable heart. In a word, we ought to try to have the "same mind as Christ Jesus." In this way, we not only "put Him on," but we acquire His very dispositions and mentality.

We ought to "communicate in all His mysteries"—that is, in the intimate dispositions of Jesus Christ in all the mysteries of His mortal, glorious, and eucharistic life. We must be small with Him in the mystery of His infancy and submissive with Him in the mystery of His youth. We must share His zeal for souls in the mystery of His public life, sacrifice ourselves with Him in the mystery of His passion, lead with Him a life of self-annihilation and adoration of the Father in the mystery of the Eucharist. Jesus lives in us as we communicate in His mysteries, and the words of St. Paul are ever more perfectly realized in us: "It is now no longer I that live, but Christ lives in me" (Gal. 2:20). It is Christ who works in me, Christ who in a certain way carries out all the acts of virtue that His grace enables me to perform during the day. It is not I, a poor creature; it is Christ in me.

In this way, "self" and self-will vanish little by little. In the place of my poor "I," Christ more and more literally invades me with His divine life. Finally, the day arrives in which truly Christ is He who lives in me, and I can say, "For me to live is Christ." The founder of the Sulpicians, the Ven. Fr. Olier, composed a little-known but beautiful invocation, which admirably sums up our relations with the incarnate Word:

> O Jesus, You who live in Mary,
> Come and live in Your servants
> with the spirit of Your holiness,
> with the fullness of Your power,
> with the perfection of Your ways,
> with the truth of Your virtues,
> with the communion of Your mysteries.
> Master all the power of the enemy with Your
> Spirit and for the glory of the Father.

Our Relations with the Father

Now, what of our relations with the Father? That which primarily characterizes Him, the first Person of the Blessed Trinity, is undoubtedly His paternity. If we could but form some idea of this paternity of God, this abyss of tenderness! As light, upon being refracted, is broken up into all the colors of the rainbow, so also the love of God, His paternity, is reflected in creatures and divided into all the many varieties of love to be seen upon the earth. When St. Paul says that all paternity in Heaven and on earth is derived from the divine paternity, he is also saying that the rich variety of love upon the earth is but a reflection of that inexhaustible fountain of love that is the paternity of God.

The divine paternity is especially reflected on earth in father and mother. Each one of us can recall those very special characteristics that mark a father and mother in the Christian home. The father is a kind of power that protects. In him we as little ones took refuge and, like the Little Flower of Jesus, never did we feel so secure as when resting in our father's lap. He is also an intelligence that directs and governs. As children we stood in awe of our father, so intelligent, talented, learned, and prudent. His opinions seemed to us the compendium of all wisdom, his decisions beyond appeal, his authority infallible. Fatherhood is also a special tenderness. A tenderness full of virility, it makes great sacrifices but does no boasting. The whole of a father's sacrifice is for his children, to educate them and assure their future; once this is assured, he dies in peace. Paternal affection surely has a character all its own.

The affection and love of a mother are of a different kind. The love of a mother is all tenderness—a tenderness that surrounds us with care our whole life through, a tenderness that sacrifices itself for us with a self-denial that knows no limits, a tenderness that envelops us in the holy caress of its love.

Now all that we admire in a Christian father and mother is infinitely deepened and multiplied in the paternity of God. God is, in a way, Father and Mother. In Him, where all perfection is fused into perfect unity, there is no division. The tenderness of God is a force in which we find protection, support, and security. A wisdom that governs and disposes all, God is also a tenderness that constantly envelops us. If we ever really understood the mystery of God's enveloping love, we should need nothing more to be intensely happy on earth.

Devotion to the Father inspired the spirituality made popular by St. Thérèse of the Infant Jesus, spiritual childhood. To regard ourselves as children of the Father is to look upon ourselves as little. As God's children, we abandon ourselves to our Father, put our confidence in Him, feel ourselves tiny in His presence. During the time that we have the happiness to possess our human parents on earth, we do not feel ourselves grown up with respect to them, nor do our parents ever consider us as grown. A child is always small, while father and mother are always big in the eyes of their children. This holds even more forcefully where God is concerned. If we feel ourselves His children, we necessarily find ourselves very little with respect to Him.

In the diary of Lucie Christine we read that one day, after Communion, she felt herself invaded by an immense tenderness. Her being seemed a drop of water lost in the ocean, an ocean of gentleness, sweetness, and tenderness. What had happened, she realized, was that the Father had "looked upon her."

The second characteristic of the Father is that He "looks." The Father brings forth the Word with an eternal look that had no beginning and will have no end. Looking upon the Word, upon the Son of His eternal complacency, through Him and in Him He looks upon all of us; in this look our being has its beginning. Upon those with a special vocation the Father has looked with a special look, which is the origin of vocation. What is a religious or priestly vocation, if not a look of predilection on the part of the Father?

If the Father looks, we can suggest that His Word is the eyes with which He looks. We know from experience what a look can mean. At times, the most eloquent words, the most finished discourses, the most inspired poetry, do not say so much as a single look. The eyes alone! They are a whole poem, a whole discourse! They can reflect an abyss of tenderness! The Father has looked upon us in just such a wonderful way. Gazing at us through His Word, or with those divine eyes that are the Word, He has looked upon us in the way that Jesus Christ looked upon the young man of whom the Gospel speaks. "And Jesus, looking upon him, loved him" (Mark 10:21). Our heavenly Father looks upon us as Jesus looked upon Mary Magdalene to transform her ... as He looked upon Peter to convert him ... as He looked upon all those who have had the happiness of being chosen for some special vocation. From this look that never departs from us, we have our life, and of it are begotten all the graces with which our soul is enriched. Yes, a characteristic of the Father is to look.

The third characteristic proper to the Father is that His is a will that governs and directs all things, but especially things in the supernatural order. Jesus Christ had no other thought during His life than to do the will of His Father, to fulfill His Father's adorable designs. St. Paul tells us that His first word on entering the world was "Behold, I come ... to do thy will, O God" (Heb. 10:7-9). His dedication to His heavenly Father moved Him to speak those words that so greatly pained Mary and Joseph, His earthly parents: "How is it that you sought me? Did you not know that I must be about my Father's business?" (Luke 2:49). These are the first words of Jesus that the Gospel quotes; and how many times He repeated them in one way or another. "My food is to do the will of him who sent me" (John 4:34). He did the will of His Father in order to glorify His Father, seeking not His own glory but only the glory of His Father.

When the supreme moment came to submerge Himself in the bitter ocean of His Passion, He told His disciples why it must be: "That the world may know that I love the Father.... Arise, let us go from here" (John 14:31). And He would not permit death to snuff out His life on earth until He cast a gaze over the whole of His life to see if any detail of His Father's will remained unfulfilled. When He saw that all had been completed, He exclaimed, "It is consummated!" (John 19:30). "I have completed the mission You gave Me to do, I have glorified You upon the earth, I have consummated Your word." There remained only for Him to drop His head upon His breast and give over His soul to His Father. "And bowing His head, He gave up his spirit" (John 19:30). The true inner being, substance, and perfection of the whole life of Jesus Christ is to fulfill completely the will of His Father in order to glorify Him.

Now our attitude toward the Father ought to be affected by the three characteristics that belong to the Father. The Father's traits should in a certain way become ours. The Father is a tenderness that loves us, a paternal tenderness that embraces in admirable unity the multitude of characteristics that love can have on earth. Therefore, our devotion to the Father ought to be an immense filial tenderness. The paternal tenderness of God ought to be the strength upon which we lean, the wisdom by which we are governed and directed, the indescribable love by which we let ourselves be loved.

If the Father's look never ceases to embrace us, then we ought to seek everywhere this look. His look is not the look of a judge, an inquisitorial look; not a look that scrutinizes, seeking out every imperfection, spying out the slightest faults in order to administer punishment. No, it is the tenderness of an indulgent Father, who better than anyone else knows our weakness and our misery. God, our Father, looks upon us to cheer and strengthen us. He looks upon us to stimulate us to try to do good and to reward us when we do. He looks upon us to pardon and transform us. In a word, He looks upon us because He loves us. All the tenderness that there is in His infinite heart He overturns, as it were, and spills upon us, in this look in which He envelops us from eternity to eternity.

And finally, if the Father is a will that governs all, a will that has a special plan for each one of us, our duty is to have no other thought but to carry out this will in everything. Our aim must be to fulfill the designs of the Father in every way and not so much to work out our own personal happiness—although this is the only way to attain it—as to glorify Him. Our Blessed Savior could say, "I do always the things that are pleasing to Him" (John 8:29). It is for us to imitate Him, always doing what the heavenly Father wishes, carrying out at every moment His designs. Our food must be to do the will of our Father who is in Heaven, seeking not our own glory but His. In every moment of our life, but above all in the difficult ones that will not be lacking, we too must say, "That the world may know that I love the Father.... Arise, let us go from here" (John 14:31). Let us go forth to carry out the will of our Father, a will that for us, as for Jesus Christ, means sacrifice of self. United with the sacrifice of Christ, our sacrifice, too, will glorify the Father.

In the prayer of all prayers, the Our Father, we are taught what our disposition toward the Father ought to be. A vocal prayer, the Our Father is also more than that. It is inexhaustible material for meditation and for the inner nourishment of the soul. Who could ever set forth all the treasures of doctrine it contains! The first part in particular, directed in a special way to the Father, reveals to us exactly what the Father should mean to us.

"Our Father, who art in Heaven." We call upon our Father who is in Heaven, in order that He may help us to do His will. In doing His will, we glorify His name. We bring about the establishment in our hearts of His kingdom, that kingdom that is joy and peace and justice in the Holy Spirit and that, after this life, will be eternal happiness. When the apostles begged Jesus to teach them to pray, He said to them, "When you pray, say: 'Father.'" Prayer, He says in effect, should above all be directed to the Father. With this in mind, a holy bishop once said that he found all spirituality contained in the "Our Father" alone.

The story is told that a certain priest once encountered in the loneliness of the countryside a young shepherd tending his flock. The shepherd was poor and uneducated. But he was a boy to whom a Christian mother had communicated that simple faith of country folk that at times puts to shame the learned. When the priest caught sight of the boy, he was perched upon a large rock, his eyes on the sheep as they wandered about the countryside, grazing freely on the grass. An air of recollection about him attracted the attention of the priest, who began to talk with him, asking him what he did during the many hours he passed in the field, with nothing in particular to occupy him. Did he not become weary and bored with so uneventful a life? The boy answered that he did not become bored. "In fact, Father, the days seem very short."

"But what is it that you do?"

"I pray."

"Pray? And what prayer do you say?"

"The Our Father. But I suppose, Father, that I really don't pray very well. Often the day is not long enough for me to recite even one Our Father. I begin, 'Our Father, who art in Heaven ...' And then I begin to think that here am I, a poor shepherd boy worth nothing, a nobody in this great big world of ours, and yet I have a Father in Heaven who loves me. My Father is so powerful that He has created all the things around me, and so good and loving toward me that He has done it all for me.

"Well, I begin to go along in this way, thinking how I am a mere nothing compared to this Father of mine. I tell Him that I love Him and that I want to be good in the way He is good ... and before I know it, my day is gone!"

Hearing of the perfect prayer of this shepherd boy, the priest could not but think of the words of Jesus to His heavenly Father: "I praise Thee, Father, Lord of heaven and earth, that Thou didst hide these things from the wise and prudent, and didst reveal them to little ones. Yes, Father, for such was Thy good pleasure" (Matt. 11:25–26). "Blessed be thou, O Father, because thus thou hast disposed it, thus thou hast sought it."

Devotion to the Father is the most fundamental of all devotions. What rest for the soul that truly understands and practices it! For all creation is truly pointed in the direction of the Father. Union with Jesus aims at taking us with Him to the Father. With profound insight, the apostle Philip exclaimed, "Lord, show us the Father and it is enough for us" (John 14:8). "Jesus, manifest the

Father to us. Grant us to know the Father. Teach us to love Him with the tenderness of children. Teach us to enfold ourselves in that look with which He has ever paternally looked upon us. Teach us to fulfill His will on earth even as it is fulfilled in Heaven.... And this is enough for us!"

Our Relations with the Holy Spirit

But it is not enough to understand our relations with the Word and with the Father. What of the Holy Spirit, the Spirit of the Father and the Son, who proceeds from both? The role of the Holy Spirit, so to speak, in the divine life is to unite the Father and the Son. The bond of union between them, He can be likened to a most close embrace, a divine kiss. The Holy Spirit consummates the divine life.

The Holy Spirit is not a principle from which any Divine Person proceeds. He rather comes to seal, to consummate in perfect unity, the life of God. For this reason, it pertains to Him to pour Himself out exteriorly for the sanctification of souls. This, as it were, is His proper role, His special mission. The Holy Spirit is not only the Spirit of the Father and the Son; He is also the Spirit of Jesus Christ as both God and man. The Holy Spirit intervenes in the whole great mystery of Christ in a very special way. First of all, the Word became incarnate in the Blessed Virgin through the work of the Holy Spirit. Moreover, the key mystery of Jesus Christ is His sacrifice. The sacrifice of Jesus explains all His other mysteries, which are like aspects or facets of the precious jewel that is His immolation. Jesus Christ did many things during His mortal life, and yet He did only one; He sacrificed. And as if it were not sufficient to fill His mortal life with sacrifices, He chose to immortalize these sacrifices in the Holy Eucharist. But this sacrifice was inspired by the Holy Spirit. For St. Paul says that "Christ ... through the Holy Spirit offered himself" (Heb. 9:14).

Now, if everything that Jesus Christ did can be reduced to His sacrifice and if His sacrifice was inspired by the Holy Spirit, then all the acts of the human life of Christ were motivated and inspired by the Holy Spirit. The Gospel tells us expressly that this was true of some of the most special and important acts in His life. For example, before beginning His life of preaching, He retired first into the desert, "led ... by the Spirit" (Matt. 4:1).

If it is the Holy Spirit who moves and directs the humanity of Jesus, and if, as we have seen, we are incorporated into that humanity, forming only one Mystical Body in a perfect, vital unity, sharing one life with Christ, then we also should be moved by the Holy Spirit. The Holy Spirit ought, consequently, to be "the soul of our soul." Our whole body is vivified by our soul, the vital principle that gives unity to our whole organism, communicates life to it, and causes each organ to have and fulfill its proper function. In the Mystical Body of Christ, the Holy Spirit is the soul. He gives life to the whole Body, governs it, directs it, moves it. He causes each one of the faithful to fulfill the *mission* entrusted to each and brings each to the degree of sanctity predestined by God according to the eternal plan.

St. Augustine asks, "Do you desire to live the life of Christ?" And he continues, "It is necessary, then, that you have the Spirit of Christ. For just as each one of my members lives with my life, because it is animated by my soul, so also the members of the Mystical Body of Christ, in order to live with His life, must be united with and animated by His Spirit, the Spirit of Christ, the Holy Spirit. If the Holy Spirit does not vivify us, direct us, move us, then we are dead members of Christ's body."

All perfection, all sanctity is here. We are saints in the measure in which the Holy Spirit governs us. We are imperfect in the measure in which we let our own proper spirit rule. We are worldly in the measure in which the spirit of the world rules us. The exceedingly perverse, the truly diabolical—and unfortunately there are some—are moved by the spirit of darkness, the devil. When we lead a self-centered, comfort-seeking, unmortified, lukewarm, lax kind of life, then our own spirit is governing us, the spirit of our fallen nature, always inclined to evil. Those whom the Holy Spirit moves with frequency are fervent souls. And those whose every action proceeds from Him are holy and perfect. Here is the whole secret of sanctity.

Now, the Holy Spirit may move us either by His inspiration or by His gifts. His inspirations, in turn, may be either illuminations or motions. Has it not happened to us at times, praying in silence, listening to the word of some preacher, reading a good spiritual book, that we have seen some already-known truth with a clarity and penetration that we never had before? The truth may be a general Christian truth, or it may be something peculiarly bearing on ourselves. The precept of fraternal charity may hit us with new force, for example, and as a kind of new insight. "Love one another as I have loved you" (John 15:12). These words, thoroughly familiar to us, today take on new meaning for us. We may not be able to explain what we felt. We cannot write a commentary on the commandment. Yet interiorly we understand it better. This is an illumination of the Holy Spirit. At other times there is a particular light regarding our own soul. During a retreat, for example, we come to realize that we are going along the wrong road, that we are becoming tepid in God's service, that we have fallen back or our forward motion is slowed. This, too, is an illumination of the Holy Spirit.

The inspirations of the Holy Spirit may also be a "motion." We not only get the light to see but we are also moved to take advantage of that light. The person who receives new understanding in the matter of fraternal charity may also feel himself moved to conduct himself in a new way, especially toward some particular person. Or again, someone who perceives that he has gone backward along the road of perfection desires efficaciously to start moving forward again. He not only sees where he ought to concentrate his efforts, but he also finds himself moved to effective action. A motion of the Holy Spirit is at work here.

Both illuminations and motions are inspirations of the Holy Spirit. They represent the ordinary manner in which He moves and directs the followers of Christ. Although the divine wisdom sweeps with great force from extreme to extreme, nevertheless it disposes of all things sweetly and with gentleness (see Wisd. 8:1). Yes, God proceeds gently with souls. Before He asks of us a sacrifice, He begins by giving us a desire for it. The desire smooths the road, makes the execution of the work easy, renders the task "natural" and spontaneous. So intimate is the action of the Holy Spirit that when we have good desires, we take them to be ours. And yet, at least in the supernatural order, there is not one good desire that comes from us alone. All are the work of the Holy Spirit, who is smoothing out difficulties and making virtue easy for us.

Now, when God gives us a desire, He proposes to see it carried out in us. Consequently, He intends to continue giving us the necessary graces until we shall have carried it out. God does not give useless desires. If through the special designs of God some particular desire is never to be carried out, then the desire itself is the work that He has asked of us. God counts as realized a good desire that we have but that we cannot carry out. St. Francis of Assisi longed ardently to preach the gospel to unbelievers. He longed even more ardently to find in his preaching an occasion of martyrdom. Francis in fact did not succeed in becoming a martyr and had to return home safe and sound. But if the will of God intended other things for Francis, God surely accepted the burning desire for the act, and St. Francis received the merit, if not the bloody crown, of the martyrs.

Now, whenever an individual is docile to the inspirations of the Holy Spirit, cooperating with grace and doing his part toward carrying out the inspiration, he performs a meritorious work that brings about an increase of grace, sanctifying him further and raising him higher on the ladder of perfection. Furthermore, seeing the person's docility, the Holy Spirit illuminates and moves him with new and more intense inspirations that otherwise he perhaps would not have received. Other inspirations come because of docility to the first. They are connected like the links of a chain. This particular inspiration may be the first link. Take hold of it and the other links will come along too. The whole series goes together. When one is faithful to inspirations, the Holy Spirit increases them more and more, in both number and intensity.

Someone who is illuminated and moved at every moment by the Holy Spirit, and who faithfully corresponds to His inspirations, cannot fail to live an active and intense spiritual life. Such a one must progress constantly in virtue, in fact veritably fly along the road of perfection. Souls are made perfect by fidelity to the Holy Spirit, the first stage in the way of perfection lying in docility to these inspirations. The Spirit rewards docility by multiplying His inspirations without measure or limit.

If on the other hand a person does not correspond to the Holy Spirit's inspirations, if he does not listen to them and is careless about them, they become rarer and rarer. St. Paul warns, "*Nolite contristare Spiritum Sanctum* — Do not grieve the Holy Spirit" (Eph.

4:30). The Holy Spirit is grieved when we let His inspirations pass us by without making use of them. Little by little He withdraws from us. If our lack of correspondence continues, the day will arrive in which He ceases to inspire us, saying nothing to us either by illumination or motion. St. Paul warns us also against this more ultimate evil: "*Spiritum nolite extinguere* — Do not extinguish the Spirit" (1 Thess. 5:19). "Let not your failure to cooperate cause the Holy Spirit to become silent and cease to work in your soul." The road of carelessness leads to lukewarmness, he warns, and even to that hardness of heart that is the prelude to final impenitence.

The second way in which the Holy Spirit moves us is by means of His *gifts*. When a person has been faithful to the inspirations of the Holy Spirit and these inspirations have been multiplied, there comes a time in which the gifts, until now almost completely latent, begin to intervene more frequently and actively. Up until this point the virtues have reigned, the virtues we exercise through our personal effort aided and supernaturalized by grace. The virtues have been exercised so far in a *human way*. This period of the spiritual life is called the "ascetical" or "active" life, or the period of "Christian asceticism." But when one has been faithful, the Holy Spirit begins to intervene in a more direct and efficacious way by means of His gifts. The period of the spiritual life in which the gifts predominate is called the "mystical life" or the "contemplative life."

In the active life, the soul itself, under the influence of grace, moves and works. In the mystical life, the soul is moved by the Holy Spirit and conducts itself passively. However, one should not suppose that under this motion of the Holy Spirit the soul remains inactive and idle. It rather enters into a new activity under the influence of the gifts and exercises the virtues in a *divine way*.

When a child in school is learning to write, he begins by making lines and circles, and then letters, and finally sentences, carefully copied from the model put before him by the teacher. He continues practicing until there results writing that is more or less satisfactory. It is a long and tedious process in which the pupil does most of the work. But there is another way of teaching to write. If this method is followed, an almost perfect letter results at once. The teacher takes the pupil's hand in order to write with it; the teacher guides the pupil's hand. In this case, rather than saying that the pupil writes, we should say that it is the teacher who writes, making use of the pupil's hand. All that is required of the pupil now is that he make no movement of his own. Entirely docile, he need only put his hand in the hand of the teacher and let the teacher make the necessary movements. A perfect letter results at once.

So there are two ways in which the Holy Spirit works in us. With His inspiration He shows us an example or model. He says to us, enlightening us, "You ought to do this," and gives us the impulse to do it. But we are the ones who do it. This is "the human way" of putting the virtues into practice.

But when the gifts come into play, the Holy Spirit does not limit Himself to inspiring the soul. He intervenes directly. He takes our faculties into His hands, so to speak, as one takes the reins of a carriage or the steering wheel of a car or the controls of an airplane. He directs the movement, and the soul conducts itself entirely passively in His hands—passively with respect to God, but extremely actively with respect to creatures. This, the "divine way" of exercising the virtues, takes place under the influence of the gifts. Virtues exercised in this way are called "perfect spiritual virtues." Their acts are called "fruits of the Holy Spirit." And when they produce in the soul a special sweetness and divine delight, they are called "Beatitudes." Just as in the example of the child and the teacher we said that it is rather the teacher who writes using the hand of the pupil, so here we can say it is rather the Holy Spirit who works using the faculties of the soul.

At this stage, there comes that exalted knowledge of God that is called "infused contemplation" because it is more of the Holy Spirit than of us, and also infused love, which belongs more to the Holy Spirit than to us. This is why the mystics say that they love through the Holy Spirit. They mean that it is the Holy Spirit who loves by means of the soul, making use of a will that has been supernaturalized by charity and an intelligence illuminated by the gift of wisdom.

We can imagine what the life of Jesus Christ as man must be like. Perfect balance, simplicity, insight, understanding, supernatural prudence—a truly perfect life! In everything, even the most insignificant details of His human life, Jesus was directed by the Holy Spirit through His gifts. From the time of Isaiah, we are taught that Jesus Christ must possess the fullness of the Holy Spirit: "And the spirit of the Lord shall rest upon him," prophesied Isaiah, "the spirit of wisdom, and of understanding, the spirit of counsel, and of fortitude, the spirit of knowledge, and of godliness. And he shall be filled with the spirit of the fear of the Lord" (Isa. 11:2-3). The fullness of the Holy Spirit rested upon Him from the first instant of the Incarnation. That is why the life of Jesus Christ was perfect.

Again, what soul can compare with the soul of the Blessed Virgin? "*Spiritus Sanctus superveniet in te*—The Holy Ghost shall come upon thee" (Luke 1:35). Not only will He come upon you, but He will come with incredible abundance, in order that you may be ruled by Him in every way. It is almost too little to say that the Blessed Virgin was docile to the inspirations of the Holy Spirit. As

St. Ephrem says, Mary was a harp played upon constantly by the Spirit. We can only imagine the harmonies that were produced, the hymns of glory to the majesty of God, the perfection in the actions that were all prompted immediately by the Spirit of God!

And yet all holy persons share a similar perfection, due proportion being preserved. For one approaches perfection and holiness in the measure in which he permits himself to be moved by the Holy Spirit. Our relations with the Holy Spirit can be summed up in terms of docility. We must place ourselves under His direction and let ourselves be moved by Him. This is the road to sanctity.

Rule 11

One of the greatest dangers for those who are trying to become holy is that of losing their first fervor and falling into lukewarmness.

The spiritual life, like the natural life, is forever threatened by illness and even by death. One of the most serious of the spiritual illnesses, if not the worst, is lukewarmness.

At first sight, it would appear useless to talk about the matter at all. Is it not generally admitted that lukewarmness is incurable? The more fervent a person is, the more he will be needlessly disturbed at the thought that he may be lukewarm. And it will never occur to the truly lukewarm individual that lukewarmness might apply to him. Genuinely lukewarm persons are spiritually deaf and blind; they are anemic and incapable of any effort. What use is there in directing any warning to them?

But in the natural order, even though we may despair of curing a sick person, we do not discontinue giving him medicine. And although a sickness be incurable, doctors do not therefore cease to study it, either in order to learn to prevent it in others or in order to attack milder cases with hope of success. So, too, in the spiritual order, lukewarmness must be studied and combated, even though we suppose it in itself incurable. There are three principal reasons.

First of all, in the supernatural order there are no strictly incurable diseases. The grace of God is all-powerful; and God, as absolute Sovereign, always keeps the last word for Himself. His mercy has resources of which we are ignorant, and His omnipotence can do all things, not only in the order of nature but also in the order of grace.

There is said to be no remedy for lukewarmness in the same sense in which it is said that the sin against the Holy Spirit does not admit of pardon. There is no specific sin that is genuinely unpardonable and that God excludes from His forgiveness; but it is possible for man obstinately to reject the grace without which there can be no true conversion or divine forgiveness. Lukewarmness is incurable in the same sense. The lukewarm person is blind. God can indeed cure him, but not realizing the state he is in, he may never seek God's cure. Moreover, the will of the lukewarm person is atrophied. If he should realize the state he is in, he is not capable of the effort required to cure himself, or he does not want to make it. What the lukewarm person needs is a special grace to enlighten and arouse him; but by his constant and willful infidelities he has rendered himself unworthy of such a grace. To say that lukewarmness is incurable is to say that the difficulty is so great that it amounts to a moral impossibility.

Second, however difficult lukewarmness may be to cure, there will always be some reason to treat of it, if only for preventive purposes. Upon realizing how serious an evil it is and how terrible are its consequences, those who are not lukewarm may be led to take precautions against it.

Finally, lukewarmness is an evil that has many degrees and takes on many forms, some serious and others mild. If it is incurable in the later stages, proper treatment in the earlier ones has all probability of success. The following considerations, then, are meant to help those who have not fallen into lukewarmness to avoid doing so, and those who have begun to take the first steps to turn back.

We shall discuss the nature of lukewarmness, its disastrous effects, its symptoms, and finally its remedies.

In What Does Lukewarmness Consist?

Lukewarmness is not exactly a sin. It is not a passing act but a state, something permanent and habitual. Its true notes are blindness and paralysis. The lukewarm person cannot see, and he is incapable of any effort.

If every fully deliberate sin tends to blind the person who commits it, attachment to sin blinds still more. Consequently, habitual and fully voluntary venial sin blinds. A lukewarm person has become attached to venial sins and commits them as naturally as one drinks water. As a result, his spiritual vision becomes cloudier and cloudier. His spirit of faith progressively diminishes until it becomes almost extinct. While the lukewarm person retains the faith necessary to avoid heresy, his faith is sluggish, theoretical, inactive, and without influence on his daily life. He has lost the esteem he once had for virtue. His attraction toward piety has disappeared along with his desires for perfection and his longings for holiness.

The lukewarm person no longer has any ideals; these ceased to exist when he became convinced that holiness was nothing but a silly illusion belonging to the years of first fervor. Now that practical life has led him to see that sanctity was not meant for him, he is content for the future to lead a life which is mediocre and common. St. Augustine saw this condition clearly and warned against it. "*Si autem dixeris: sufficit, periisti*—When you say, 'I have done enough,' you are lost."

As our willing naturally follows our knowing, this blindness of the understanding has as its necessary consequence an ever accentuated weakening of the will. The Gospel speaks of certain sick persons whom it calls "languid" (*curavit languidos*) (Matt. 14:14) and of a sickness that it calls "languidity" (*sanans omnem languorem*) (Matt. 4:23). Lukewarmness is such a sickness in the supernatural order. The will has lost the fervor, the enthusiasm, the fine temper of better days. Having ceased to fight, it languishes prostrate, without elasticity, without spirit, incapable of any effort, in a state of spiritual anemia that at times amounts to a true paralysis.

The two characteristic traits of lukewarmness, then, are blindness of the intellect and paralysis of the will.

In order that the intellect may see, and the will move, there are required illuminating and strengthening graces. But the lukewarm person renders himself unworthy of these graces by his constant and habitual infidelity. God's efficacious grace does not come, and the soul remains in darkness and helplessness. The cause of lukewarmness, then, is a progressive infidelity to grace, manifested primarily by negligence in the service of God. The lukewarm person never makes *fervent* acts of virtue, that is, acts that reach up to the level of grace already attained. He rather makes *remiss* acts: imperfect, careless, tepid acts, less intense than the grace he already possesses. His practices of piety, which are the nourishment of the soul, he makes with negligence. His prayer is full of voluntary distractions, his examen superficial, his Communion routine. And this negligence is not transitory but habitual and voluntary.

The lukewarm person may soon go further. Not only does he perform his religious duties carelessly, but soon he begins to shorten them and will use the slightest pretext to eliminate them. How often will he not allege motives that are in themselves irreproachable—for example, works of charity on behalf of his neighbor! He salves his conscience, saying that after all he is only "leaving God for God." But what is happening is that activity is increasingly supplanting prayer.

The devil knows well that it would be a waste of time to try directly to induce fervent souls to sin. His strategy is to lead such persons progressively to increase their external works and activities, with prejudice to their religious obligations. Almost imperceptibly he brings it about that prayer is eliminated, so that there remains an activity without any soul to it, a purely exterior and human activity that is sterile, fruitless, and even harmful. Without nourishment from his religious exercises, a person becomes spiritually weakened; and as an anemic organism is a propitious field for the growth of harmful germs, so the soul without prayer is disposed for the germination of disordered affections.

When inordinate affections are allowed free play, they inevitably produce the fruit of deliberate and habitual venial sin. This is the third stage of lukewarmness, or lukewarmness at its worst. The horror of sin is gone; a person willfully commits whatever venial sins present themselves, without his conscience either becoming alarmed or protesting. To this state of indifference comes a soul called to perfection!

Disastrous Effects of Lukewarmness

The description in the preceding section is sufficient of itself to show us the gravity of lukewarmness. It is certainly no trifle for a person to be blind and paralyzed with respect to spiritual things, for his understanding to be insensible to them and his will incapable of the slightest effort to attain them. But this is not the whole story. All of the evil effects of lukewarmness, many as they are, can be reduced to one principal evil in which all the others are contained and from which they flow. This principal evil we may describe as the attitude of God toward the lukewarm soul.

Our Lord Himself has told us what God's attitude is. A code of mercy and pardon, of confidence and peace, the New Testament nevertheless contains warnings of extraordinary rigor. And perhaps the severest warning in it concerns lukewarmness. Directing Himself to the lukewarm person, Jesus utters the following frightful rebuke: "I know thy works; thou art neither cold nor hot. I would that thou wert cold or hot. But because thou art lukewarm, and neither cold nor hot, I am about to vomit thee out of my mouth; because thou sayest, 'I am rich and have grown wealthy and have need of nothing,' and dost not know that thou art the wretched and miserable and poor and blind and naked one" (Rev. 3:15–17). What, we ask ourselves, can be the import of such terrible words, referring, as they undoubtedly do, to lukewarmness in its ultimate and most serious degree? At first sight, our Lord seems to prefer mortal sin itself to lukewarmness: "I would that thou wert cold or hot"—that is, fervent or a sinner—"and not lukewarm." If it is absurd to suppose that our Lord really hates mortal sin less than venial, what precisely is the meaning of His dire warning to the lukewarm?

Considering these words first as they apply to the good and fervent, we can affirm that, for the good, lukewarmness is, in a certain sense, more dangerous than mortal sin. Mortal sin of itself alarms, disgusts, horrifies. Those who fear God place themselves instinctively on guard against mortal sin and try to remove themselves as far as possible from its occasions. Their attitude toward lukewarmness, especially considered in its earlier stages, is likely to be different. Small infidelities do not so much alarm the conscience as put it to sleep. As a result, there is a real danger that a good person may fall into lukewarmness almost without noticing it. Since mortal sin is a manifest and brazen enemy, while lukewarmness is a crafty and hypocritical one, the good may have to be more on guard against lukewarmness than against mortal sin.

Rule 11

Also for the less fervent, lukewarmness may be in a certain sense more dangerous than mortal sin. When a person sins seriously because of weakness and misery rather than because of malice, he can with relative ease get out of the state of sin, turn sincerely to God, and begin to lead a life of fervor. How many times do people sin because they are ignorant of the gravity of sin and are not aware of all that Jesus Christ has done and suffered in order to obtain for them the divine pardon! Many sources can be successfully tapped to obtain the conversion of the sinner. One can appeal to the seriousness of sin, the four last things, the Passion of our Savior, and many other themes. Moreover, as the ordinary sinner may have received relatively few graces, he cannot be said to have systematically and deliberately abused grace. God is disposed to bestow graces generously on the ordinary sinner, whose conversion can at times be definitive and is always sincere.

The situation with the lukewarm is quite different. Lukewarmness is not an illness of beginners. It presupposes a more or less lengthy period of fervor and abundant graces. It touches persons who know the gravity of sin, who have meditated much on the eternal truths and on the Passion of our Savior, who through personal experience have tasted the sweetness of divine love. A lukewarm person is one who has had these graces, who has blinded and paralyzed himself spiritually, and has become deaf to divine inspirations and insensible to earnest exhortations. The lukewarm has made himself unworthy of God's grace, and there remain no resources to be tapped. As a result of the abuse of His grace, God has taken it away. A lukewarm person's return to fervor is therefore so difficult that we can say that it is morally impossible in the sense explained above.

Although mortal sin is incomparably more serious than venial, a person in the state of mortal sin can turn to God with relative ease. But when lukewarmness is found in its most serious degree, it is morally impossible for a soul to recover. From this point of view, is it not better to be cold than lukewarm? "I would that thou wert cold or hot."

The words that follow are truly terrible on the lips of our Lord, always so merciful to the sinner. They have a realism that any comment on them tends to soften. "But because thou art lukewarm, and neither cold nor hot, I am about to vomit thee out of my mouth." With this expression, which may appear dull to the blunted sensibilities of our day, our Lord wants to make clear how repugnant to Him lukewarmness is. Consider Jesus' attitude toward different sorts of people. Toward the good, He feels tenderness and gentleness; toward the sinful, forgiveness, compassion, and mercy; but for the lukewarm He feels a repugnance and nausea like that of one about to vomit. Does not this in itself represent the supreme punishment for lukewarmness?

Whenever God loves, He loves most actively. His love is manifested in the abundance of His gifts, so that souls are literally overwhelmed by the greatness of divine love. When God has mercy, He seems to forget His own dignity, lowering Himself to the sinner and seeking him out in the abyss of his offenses. And when, after knocking for a long time at the door of some heart and never tiring, He at last finds it opened to Him, His joy is greater than that which He would feel over the perseverance of ninety-nine just.

Now what happens when God is nauseated by a soul? This is something so frightening and mysterious that one scarcely dares to sound it out. Would this revulsion be an abandonment by God similar, if only remotely so, to the definitive abandonment with which God casts off the reprobate and permits him to be buried in the abyss of eternal hate? To say so much would seem to be going too far.

Undoubtedly, God never abandons anyone definitively in this life. He always offers graces at least sufficient for salvation; never is salvation in this world absolutely impossible, and damnation is always inexcusable. Nevertheless, God does in some sense abandon the lukewarm person. Because of the soul's unworthiness, God withdraws the graces of election that otherwise He would have given.

Lukewarmness involves unfaithfulness; unfaithfulness supposes a friendship betrayed, a love unrequited. If faithfulness is perseverance in love, unfaithfulness is a love that has grown weary, a friendship that has failed. It is represented by a loved one who has turned his back. Now will not our own hearts tell us that the unfaithfulness of a friend causes much more pain than grave injustice from a stranger? An affront by a stranger insults our dignity and damages our rights; but unfaithfulness on the part of a friend rends its most delicate fibers. When a friend betrays us, we know that as Christians we ought to forgive him. But no one obliges us to renew the friendship that has been betrayed; perhaps it would even be impossible.

Does something like this take place between God and the soul? Magnanimous in everything, God undoubtedly is ready to renew the former friendship. Divine love never admits defeat. But the soul, through its own fault, has made itself incapable of that love. For this reason, it appears as if God has in fact abandoned the soul definitively, turned His back on it as on a thing that makes one want to vomit.

Can a lukewarm soul be saved? Before answering this terrible question, let us not forget something we set down in the beginning—namely, that we are here treating of lukewarmness in its most extreme degree. Speaking even of this lukewarmness, we must still say that a lukewarm person, absolutely speaking, can be saved; sufficient graces are not wanting to him. On the other hand, granted that state of blindness and spiritual anemia in which he finds himself through his own fault, ordinary graces in fact are not sufficient for his salvation. A most efficacious grace is needed to jolt him and draw him out of his stupor. And how will God give this special grace if with repeated infidelities he has made himself unworthy of it?

In fact, a person will not generally remain merely lukewarm. Lukewarmness is not generally a permanent state but a passing one, a phase through which a person goes as he descends from his first fervor. Now, a basic principle of the spiritual life is that no one can remain stationary. Either he progresses and keeps going higher, or he backslides and keeps going down until he buries himself in the abyss of habitual mortal sin. A lukewarm person is characterized by affection for venial sins; he commits them constantly and ever increasingly. But if habitual and completely voluntary, venial sin weakens the soul and numbs the conscience, in this way predisposing for mortal sin. Moreover, the boundary between mortal and venial sin frequently cannot be defined with precision, and when one is constantly approaching this boundary, he is someday very likely to cross it. His conscience becomes so relaxed that it makes no protest upon seeing the soul stained by some serious fault; when it does protest, its complaint is quieted.

Now constant unfaithfulness to grace results in its withdrawal. God withdraws His graces more and more, abandoning the individual to his own resources. And in these circumstances, of what is he not capable? What sin may he not commit? Into what abyss may he not plunge? The devil, moreover, has but been awaiting the moment most favorable to his designs. At the right moment, he sets up a strong temptation and the lukewarm person falls. These falls become multiplied, and there results a habitual state of mortal sin — a thousand times worse if this state is combined with a series of sacrilegious Confessions and Communions.

Now, the circumstances of someone who has always been sinful are very different from those of a lukewarm soul that has become sinful. As the first has not abused the grace of God, he can easily receive the grace of conversion. But the latter has left no point at which he is easily vulnerable to God's grace. Moreover, he has made himself unworthy of the especially efficacious grace he needs to draw him from the abyss in which he has been buried. There remains only the frightful threat of Jesus: "Because thou art lukewarm, and neither cold nor hot, I am about to vomit thee out of my mouth" (Rev. 3:16).

Most terrible of all, the lukewarm person, too blind for self-knowledge, does not realize the state he is in. As he maintains certain exterior expressions of piety, he deceives himself into believing that he is rich in virtues, abundant in merits, and in need of nothing. But the truth is so completely to the contrary that Jesus hurls into his face the terrible words: "Thou ... dost not know that thou art the wretched and miserable and poor ... and naked one" (Rev. 3:17).

How to Know Whether a Soul Is in a State of Lukewarmness

It is extremely important to have sure and exact rules that can be of service in discerning whether someone is lukewarm. First, we should remember that lukewarmness is not an illness of beginners and that it always comes after a period of fervor, an appreciable period of fervor, enthusiasm, and fidelity in God's service. From such a first fervor, a person descends to lukewarmness by degrees. Infrequent and insignificant in the beginning, his infidelities become more frequent and aggravated later on. In the physical or natural order, lukewarmness is a state midway between cold and hot. A thing must pass through it whether the temperature be going up or down. What is cold becomes lukewarm and then hot; what is hot becomes lukewarm and finally cold. The same principle does not hold in the supernatural order. Spiritual lukewarmness is a decline, a degradation, and one arrives at it only by going down. From fervor a person descends to lukewarmness; from lukewarmness to mortal sin; and from isolated mortal sin he descends to the vice or habit of mortal sin.

There is a state superficially similar to lukewarmness, which nevertheless must be carefully distinguished from it. This state is spiritual dryness or aridity. Like lukewarmness, spiritual aridity comes after a period of fervor, and in it all sensible fervor is absent. Yet the two states are completely opposed, spiritual aridity being a step forward, lukewarmness a step backward.

To foster detachment from creatures and attachment to works of piety in beginners, God frequently grants sensible consolation in His service. But although helpful in the beginning, sensible consolations in prayer can be harmful over an extended period. As we become attached to them, they will prevent us from living by pure faith and will hinder our love from being pure and disinterested. It is really as a reward for fidelity and as a sign of progress, then, that God withdraws sensible devotion in order that we may learn in dryness to live by faith and to love God disinterestedly. In aridity we preserve our fear of offending God, our desire to love Him, and our longing to reach perfection. It pains us to see ourselves in this state of helplessness; and if we can find no comfort in the things of God, neither do we find it in creatures.

The lukewarm person is very different. He more and more loses all fear of sin, his charity grows cold, his desires for perfection become nil. These characteristics become accentuated as his lukewarmness grows. Far from being pained at discovering himself in this state, he is satisfied to be as he is. Not realizing the serious-ness of his condition, he does nothing to get out of it. He has no taste for the works of piety. Spiritual things weary him. He cannot live without comforts and satisfactions; and not finding these in God, he seeks them in creatures, to which he becomes inordinately attached. Spiritual dryness differs from lukewarmness, then, as night from day.

A second sign of lukewarmness is carelessness about prayers and spiritual exercises. We are speaking here not of an incidental but of a habitual and constant carelessness, a carelessness, moreover, that is willful and deliberate. An effort always sustained at the heights, with no eclipse or faltering whatsoever, is more than heroic and far above ordinary human powers. Such a prodigy of constancy and fidelity we can admire in the Blessed Virgin. But hers was a singular privilege. Granted our human weakness and misery, there is no one of us, however good he be, who does not have days or hours of dejection. The mark of real spiritual earnestness does not lie in never faltering but in quickly rallying and again pushing forward.

Lukewarmness is quite different from this inevitable human weakness. The lukewarm person carries out all his spiritual duties carelessly, negligently, hastily, and wearily, while at the same time displaying in the whole natural order a marvelous diligence and activity. His spiritual negligence is not the product of an apathetic temperament or lazy character, since it is in sharp contrast to his diligence in material and human things.

How will this negligence express itself practically? In a thousand ways in daily life. The lukewarm person may be unfaithful to the appointed time for getting up in the morning—he remains in bed as long as he can. He habitually and voluntarily indulges distractions and idleness at time of prayer, if he does not sleep the allotted time away altogether. Lacking both preparation and thanksgiving, his Communions bear no fruit. Whenever he can, he postpones Confession; and when he goes, his Confessions are superficial, without true sorrow and real purpose of amendment, his sole purpose in going being to avoid some greater inconvenience.

He never carries out any examination of conscience. Why should he? He has no desire to know himself, and he has no intention of changing his ways. Spiritual reading he finds boring and tiresome; he prefers light, frivolous, and even dangerous reading. Rather than practice any penance, he seeks in everything his own convenience. Instead of mortifying himself in the matter of food, he gives free rein to his taste in both quantity and quality. His prayers are recited mechanically and with haste; routine is the order of the day in his spiritual exercises. As lukewarmness increases, not only are religious exercises performed negligently, but they are also shortened and abandoned on the slightest pretext. When we pray badly, prayer wearies us; and when prayer wearies us, we are tempted to abandon it.

The first practices abandoned are those that require more effort, such as the daily examen, weekly Confession, meditation; or those that are more austere, such as practices of mortification. Since spiritual exercises are the food of the soul, when they are done badly or eliminated, the soul gets weaker and weaker, becoming rickety, anemic, and incapable of any effort. This, as we have said, is the salient characteristic of a lukewarm individual.

A third sign of lukewarmness is the desire to avoid mortal sin only. The fervent person fears not only mortal sin but venial sin as well. Venial sin, because an offense against God, he sees as "mortal for the heart." When through frailty he falls, he repents at once and tries to avoid future falls. He especially tries to avoid fully deliberate venial sins and is always hard at work to uproot previously contracted evil habits.

The lukewarm person is just the opposite. If he still fears clear and obvious mortal sin, this is only because he fears Hell. As for venial sin, he almost welcomes it and seems to take a certain delight in it. Committing venial sins with full advertence and as often as the occasion presents itself, he fosters bad habits that in turn enslave him more and more. The most characteristic note of lukewarmness is the habit of sinning venially, with pleasure, without remorse, and without the remotest intention of amendment. The conscience of the lukewarm person is insensible, too relaxed in one respect and quite hardened in another. Disgust for sin is a grace; but the lukewarm soul has so abused God's grace, despising all salutary movements of regret, that God ends up by withdrawing even a sense of remorse. The lukewarm person can sin with gusto and affection, sin having become for him a kind of pastime. Looking upon himself as a mind of very broad standards and very much abreast of the times, he ridicules "pious souls" who try to avoid venial sins and lead a life that even in small things conforms to the precepts of Christian morality. To him, the conscientious servants of our Savior are a scrupulous, straitlaced, timorous lot. Poor soul! What good reason Jesus has to say to him, "I know thy works; thou hast the name of being alive [because you acquired it in your years of fervor], and thou art dead" (Rev. 3:1).

The Remedies

When we ask about the possibility of one who has fallen into lukewarmness getting out of this state and returning to a life of fervor, we must distinguish three stages of lukewarmness or three classes of lukewarm souls. Some are in the worst stages of lukewarmness, some have only just entered the earlier stages, and some, without being properly lukewarm, are nevertheless in danger of becoming so.

As for the worst stages, we have already seen that it can be said to be morally impossible to recover from them and return to a life of fervor. Conversion requires an extraordinary grace from God that these individuals do not deserve and will neither ask nor desire. Spiritually blind, they just barely keep the faith necessary to avoid heresy or unbelief, an inactive and atrophied faith that has no influence in their lives. As a consequence of their blindness, they become more and more insensible until they arrive at a hardness of heart similar to that which prepares the hardened sinner for final impenitence. In fact, they themselves are on the verge of falling into habitual mortal sin.

Is their case one for utter despair? Fortunately not, for there is a possible solution in the consoling doctrine of the communion of saints. If there is somewhere someone who will take an interest in these poor lukewarm souls, vicarious prayers and sacrifices can obtain from the divine mercy the needed extraordinary grace of conversion. Who will be such a helper in the life of some particular individual? Perhaps a near relative who has noted the extreme lukewarmness of this dear one. Perhaps a friend — and what better service of Christian friendship than this? Perhaps it will be some sister or cloistered nun, who, if she has consecrated her life to prayer and sacrifice for sinners, certainly has not to exclude the lukewarm whose need may in a certain sense be greater. It may be a zealous and holy priest who, having noticed in the confessional the state of certain penitents and gaining nothing by exhortation, resorts to prayer and penance in order to win them and soften their hearts.

At times, too, the divine mercy, always in search of pretexts and occasions for pouring itself out upon even the most poorly disposed, will find in the lukewarm individual himself something that in a certain sense justifies the extraordinary grace of conversion. It may be an extraordinary deed in the person's past life, some great act of charity, an important service done for the Church, or some great sacrifice. It may be a devotion or practice of piety, especially to the Sacred Heart or the Blessed Virgin, which in the midst of so much wretchedness has been conserved like a glowing ember underneath the ashes.

We may add that once God has granted the efficacious grace that shakes up, jolts, and transforms the soul, nothing is so much called for as a closed retreat, with a general confession of the whole period of lukewarmness.

Less serious lukewarmness can be more directly reached by human aid. The Gospel narrative of St. John tells us of the cure of a paralytic by the pool of Siloe. This man had been waiting thirty-eight years for a cure. He had not attained it, because as he sadly told our Savior, "Sir, I have no one to put me into the pool when the water is stirred" (John 5:7). Paralytic that he was, he had not the power in himself to get down into the water when the angel miraculously moved it.

The lukewarm person is like that paralytic. Spiritually paralyzed, he needs someone to help him, someone with divine power to say, "Rise, take up thy pallet and walk" (John 5:8). More specifically, he needs the service of a zealous confessor who will efficaciously help him to get rid of his malady not only by general exhortations and counsels but also by means accommodated to his particular needs. While this is not the place to treat in detail of how the confessor should proceed, we shall indicate the general means for helping souls to rise out of incipient lukewarmness.

First, the lukewarm individual must be convinced that he is lukewarm. Misled regarding his true state of soul, he supposes that because he does not fall into serious sin he must be spiritually quite sound. But a little reflection in God's presence, and with good will, will bring out the contrast between his earlier years of fervor and his present carelessness. Comparing seriously and earnestly the one period with the other, he cannot but see that instead of advancing he has gone backward. If he consults an experienced confessor, preferably one who knows him well, such a confessor will confirm and reinforce his fears, at the same time assuring him that there is still time to escape.

Now once he is convinced, how is he to be cured? When a doctor sets out to cure someone, he is not content to attack the symptoms, as a simple palliative might do; he seeks out the cause of the symptoms and attacks this. This is how one must proceed against lukewarmness, for with lukewarmness, too, identical characteristic effects may originate in different immediate causes.

Lukewarmness may originate in some inordinate affection, which, encouraged rather than combated, now flourishes like a great parasite and absorbs all the vital energies of the soul. When a man has become spiritually anemic and nothing in the spiritual order attracts him, the only way he can return to fervor is to fight against the inordinate affection that is the cause of his trouble and implacably root it out of his heart.

Or again, lukewarmness may be traceable to some defect that an individual has failed to fight and that has continued to grow and develop until it has become a habit. For example, a person may indulge the habit of lying and deceiving until he has created a whole life of duplicity and pretense. Or he may have cultivated the habit of seeking in everything his own convenience and of flying from any and all mortification, the habit of complaining about everyone and everything. He may have developed such a flippancy, or a lack of reflection, deliberation, and judgment, that he can take nothing seriously and must look at everything superficially. He may have gotten into the habit of chattering endlessly, monopolizing every conversation, yet never saying anything profitable, but simply speaking of himself, extolling his own actions, and boasting of his own exploits. Each of these instances manifests the most characteristic note of lukewarmness, the voluntary habit of venial sin. Anybody who wishes to fight free of lukewarmness will have to struggle earnestly against the defect that caused him to fall into it.

Finally, lukewarmness can arise simply from a general carelessness and negligence in the carrying out of spiritual exercises. Prayer, Mass, Communion, spiritual reading, examination of conscience, Confession become routine. But since spiritual exercises are the food of the soul, the spiritual organism becomes anemic when they are done badly or are omitted. The only way to recovery of health is to return to the conscientious performance of one's religious duties.

In doing this, one must avoid the danger of trying to do everything at once, as if all the old energies could be recovered in a single moment. A person just emerging from a serious illness does not instantaneously recover his full strength, convalescence often being longer and requiring more delicate care than the illness itself. Since the lukewarm person is spiritually anemic, he comes out of his lethargy with a minimum of strength of will. He must therefore adjust the object of his efforts to the littleness of his energies, and as his strength increases, he can undertake more difficult tasks. If he tries to do more than he is able and fails, he will let everything go and return to his lukewarmness.

Someone who has been careless about spiritual exercises, for example, is not to set himself the task from the very first moment of doing all of them perfectly. Let him take them one by one. He can begin with prayer and concentrate all his efforts on doing this well. He can even limit his aim to fighting distractions. Or if he is accustomed to half an hour of mental prayer, let him begin by working at actual mental prayer for only fifteen minutes, devoting the other fifteen minutes to spiritual reading or vocal prayers.

Someone who is not strictly lukewarm but is in danger of becoming lukewarm can even more opportunely make use of the means indicated above. Prevention is better than cure. But it should be remembered that slight lukewarmness or the danger of falling into it is not to be confused with a state pathological rather than moral. Because of excessive work (especially intellectual), great trials, or a general run-down condition, someone may suffer a noticeable depression, lack of energy, loss of willpower — a complete enervation of will, so that he does not seem to have the strength to do anything at all. But where these are the causes, a doctor is needed rather than a priest.

There are also spiritually wounded souls, who are not to be confused with the lukewarm. Excessively severe humiliations, flagrant injustices, or failures sometimes crush a whole life. When great trials swoop down upon a person who is not of an almost heroic temper, they sometimes shatter him and may ruin him completely. Overwhelmed by discouragement, he develops a kind of spiritual inferiority complex. His faith and confidence in others and in himself are gone. No longer caring about anything, he with great difficulty drags himself along in a life that looks to him completely meaningless. Such an individual is fortunate if he finds along his path a priest according to the heart of God, who, like the Good Samaritan, binds his wounds, restores his strength, and causes to shine anew from the depths of his depression the light of the divine ideal of perfection. After all, even the most humiliating cross is a royal road that leads to God. God, who never deceives, is the supreme reason for our life and its ultimate meaning, even when humanly it appears shattered. The spiritually shattered individual must be treated with kindness and understanding, not severity.

In closing, let us take a look at a typical historical case that will show not only that God can but that in fact He does cure lukewarm souls and even raise them to sanctity. Perhaps the fact that this is a saint who is little known to us will make the example all the more impressive. At the end of the sixteenth century there was in Italy a family of noble lineage, the Mariscotti family, probably of Scottish origin and descended from Marius Scotus, who established himself in Italy in the time of Charlemagne. A member of this family married into the famous Orsini family, and the couple had three daughters. All three received a Christian education, and the eldest found her vocation as a Franciscan religious in the Convent of San Bernardino of Viterbo. The second daughter, Clara, was an extremely difficult girl and the nightmare of her parents. When her younger sister, Hortensia, made an excellent family match, Clara considered herself disgraced that a younger sister should have been asked for in marriage before herself. So great was her spite at this humiliation that she determined to enter the Convent of San Bernardino, without so much as considering the real meaning of vocation. She could not, of course, have committed a more serious error than thus embracing the religious life without a supernatural motive.

With such a motive for entering, we can imagine the life of Clara in the convent. The rule, the common life, the religious spirit all meant nothing to her. Abusing her family influence and certain special traits of the community, she managed to have her cell furnished with every comfort in complete contradiction to Franciscan poverty. She even had special food brought in, justifying the irregularity by a variety of pretexts. For ten years, she lived this disedifying life. Then, perhaps through the prayers of the community and especially of her sister, a religious in the same convent, the hand of God intervened. God first sent sickness. To hear the sick nun's confession, her confessor had to enter her cell, and on seeing its luxury he realized what an unfortunate state Clara was in. God put such efficacy into this man's exhortation that Clara's heart was moved, and from that day her conversion began.

Clara recovered from this illness only to fall into another, longer and more serious, which put her at death's door. The brush with death completed the work already begun, and Clara arose from her bed a different person. She began to live a life of humility, penance, poverty, strict observance, and fraternal charity that was a marvel to the whole community. The sixteenth century was a time of severe penances, and Clara would be outdone by no one. Her bed was a bare board, her pillow a rock. She habitually wore a hair shirt. She took the discipline until she was bloody; she wore on her head a band bristling with thorns, and she fasted frequently on bread and water. In compensation for Clara's newfound generosity, God led her along the ways of prayer until she reached the highest union with Him. To witness to her virtue, He favored her with the extraordinary gifts of counsel, miracles, and prophecy. When Clara died at the age of fifty-five, in the year 1640, she was a saint.

The Church has placed her on its altars and venerates her under the name of St. Hyacinth Mariscotti. It was the name given to her in the Convent of San Bernardino, where for ten years she led a lukewarm life, and for many more years a fervent and holy one.

Rule 12

The essential law of the spiritual life, as of all life, is progress and growth. The alternative is decay and death.

Souls are hungry for God! In the midst of a materialism that looks only to money and pleasure, men, surfeited by the false goods of the world, are resolutely turning to God. This reaction can be seen among people of every sort: among the cultivated and learned as also among the ignorant and unlettered; among those who by God's special providence have preserved their baptismal innocence as also among the prodigals who are returning from distant lands to the house of their father in search of pardon and peace; among the rich, who, favored by fortune and living in abundance, are able to drink from the cup of every pleasure, as also among the poor, who, disinherited by fortune, eat a bread kneaded with tears and sweat; among those in the first years of life as well as among those who, disillusioned with earth, are descending the slope that terminates in the grave.

Yes, everywhere one finds this thirst for God, for the spirit blows where it will (see John 3:8). But if this necessity for God is found everywhere, in some places it reaches gigantic proportions, whether in souls consecrated to God in the cloister or in devout persons in the world who are striving to practice virtue and arrive at perfection. Impoverished and spiritually stingy indeed are those who do not suffer this hunger for God!

Now, uncertainty often causes real anguish in those who are trying to lead a spiritual life and who have a burning desire to be united with God. "Am I going forward along the road that leads to God?" they wonder. "Am I perhaps going backward? Or am I simply standing still?" This problem becomes aggravated if in spite of spending years in working to correct a defect—for example, to acquire humility, patience, meekness—the defect still persists in a most discouraging way. As the habitual defect persists, the person naturally falls more or less frequently into more or less deliberate faults.

This persistence of defects is very naturally taken as an indication that no progress is being made. How can faults and falls continue in spite of the sincerest will to overcome them? If after years of working to correct a defect, the defect seems just as lively as ever, a person naturally concludes that his spiritual life must have become stagnant. And if, as sometimes happens, he passes through one of those periods when a defect becomes aggravated and is actually more troublesome than in an earlier period, he concludes that instead of progressing he must surely be going backward. How easy it is in these circumstances for discouragement to enter in! Deceived by the devil, how readily one will abandon the work of sanctification, bitterly concluding that holiness is not for him!

In order to solve this problem, we must first of all limit its scope. There are not three alternatives, but two. One must go either forward or backward, since, practically speaking, standing still in the spiritual life is impossible according to a universally admitted spiritual principle. The spiritual life is a true life. And no life in this world can stand still, for it is either an activity and a developing, or it is a decaying and a movement toward death. In human life we see first a ceaseless progress from infancy until maturity; and afterward we see a steady decline that culminates in death. More palpably, we see this law in our sensitive life, where not for one moment does the heart cease to beat, the blood to circulate, the lungs to respire, or any one of the various organs fail to fulfill its proper vital functions.

Just as there is no middle ground between sickness and health, though health can be more or less vigorous and illness more or less serious, so also and more emphatically there can be no middle ground in the spiritual life. The soul either possesses the grace of God or it is in the state of sin. Now, if a person is in a state of grace, he merits, however little it may be, and consequently he progresses. If he is in the state of sin, he is dead, and like a corpse he is in the process of decomposition.

The problem, then, can be reduced to this: to know whether one is going forward or backward. Is the persistence of defects and of falls a sign of going backward? The answer depends on whether the individual in question is trying or not. When someone fails to avoid falls or correct his faults because he is not making the required effort, he is not advancing but going backward. With each new fall, a bad habit is becoming more ingrained, a defect taking deeper root.

We must not forget that defects and virtues are intimately connected with their respective acts as cause with effect. A habit tends to produce its proper acts. When a habit is present, the respective act is performed with frequency and ease. A defect, as a bad habit, tends to produce corresponding bad acts. Moreover, these bad acts are performed with progressively greater frequency and ease. The person who is naturally hot-tempered, for example, and who does not struggle to correct his defect, will be found to give in to his temper more and more readily.

Now, what of a person who does struggle? Suppose that in spite of years of effort he finds himself with the same defects he had at the beginning? The most natural thing in the world is for him to become increasingly discouraged. His effort seems completely useless. Discouragement ever more naturally holds sway when the same defects not only continue but even increase.

Before we answer this question, there are several points that need to be clarified. First, our defects and falls have their immediate cause in our will. God, who has nothing to do with them except to permit them, exercises no direct causality upon them. The Highest Good cannot be the cause of any evil, nor can anything unholy proceed from Supreme Holiness. Circumstance, environment, education, heredity, can exercise influence for good or bad; but the cause of our defects and falls is our will. No defect or fault can be imputed to us except in the measure in which we will it. Where the will does not intervene, the moral order does not exist.

Second, we must remember that our will is not the cause of our acquiring supernatural virtues. At first sight, this assertion may appear strange or even scandalous to the pious. We are so accustomed to believe that the supernatural virtues are acquired and increased with the repetition of acts just as the natural virtues are! Natural habits, it is true, are acquired and increased by repeated acts. But supernatural habits or virtues are not. These are essentially infused, and their very name indicates that man does not acquire them but that God infuses them. Now, the same cause that gives birth to a virtue makes it grow. It is a truth of faith that man in a state of mortal sin cannot by his own efforts acquire either grace or the infused virtues and gifts of the Holy Spirit inseparable from it. Consequently, he cannot by his own personal effort or his own acts acquire or increase grace; nor can he acquire or increase the supernatural virtues.

It can be objected that although man cannot by his own effort put himself in the state of grace and acquire the virtues, once he has been placed in grace his acts are supernatural, and he can with these cause the virtues to increase. In answer to this, it must be remembered that grace and the supernatural virtues are a participation in the divine nature and activity. Beyond the reach of man, even when he is elevated to the supernatural order, they always remain a free gift of God. It is God who infuses grace and increases it, God who infuses the virtues and causes them to grow. This is why the Church teaches us to ask this gift of God: "*Da nobis fidei, spei, et caritatis augmentum*—Give us increase of faith, hope, and charity."

On the other hand, it would be a serious mistake to conclude that if my efforts do not produce the increase of the virtues, then it is useless to try. No response could be more unwarranted than to fold one's hands in lazy inactivity. For if one's own efforts and acts of virtue do not properly produce the increase of supernatural virtues, inasmuch as they are not the efficient cause of the increase, they are the necessary condition that God has set down for that increase to take place.

Our efforts in the state of grace are, practically speaking, acts of virtue, and they produce merit. They are meritorious acts. Now, merit is the right that the soul acquires before God to the increase of grace and the virtues, and to eternal glory in the life to come. In short, God confers the infused virtues and their increase; man does not acquire them. But man has to place the conditions prescribed by God, which conditions in practice are nothing else but the effort to practice the virtues and correct defects.

Third, we must understand that when this necessary condition has been placed, grace and the virtues increase without fail, for God does not contradict Himself. The Church teaches us that every good act done in the state of grace merits an increase of grace and of glory. Now, the virtues and gifts must increase in a parallel manner, because they all form one spiritual living whole that grows harmoniously as the body of a child grows to maturity.

Finally, this increase is not sensible. Frequently, it cannot be verified and remains quite hidden. God so loves humility that in order to teach a soul humility He may permit it to fall seriously. Or with more likelihood, He will permit exterior manifestations of a defect to persist for a long time, even for a whole lifetime. Although now the person no longer consents to it, the defect will appear to remain without correction, or even to be aggravated at times.

St. Vincent de Paul struggled constantly and generously for years against a melancholy disposition that gave his countenance an air of severity and harshness, which, instead of attracting others, repelled them. St. Francis de Sales, by disposition hot-tempered, struggled for many years against this disposition without ceasing to feel its movements. When he succeeded in conquering its exterior manifestations, he still experienced it interiorly. On one occasion, when someone had insulted him without his showing any anger, he was later asked in confidence if he hadn't felt even a little emotion. He answered, "I felt anger boiling in my brain like a kettle on a fire." St. Bernadette was by nature timid and highly impressionable. Certain traces of the original rusticity of her childhood stayed with her almost her whole life and in part gave occasion to the dislike felt toward her by her superior.

Especially in order to keep souls in humility, God permits them to fall not only into involuntary and semideliberate smaller faults but even into more serious ones. Confirmation in grace is a wonderful favor that God bestows only on souls that have arrived at the pinnacle of holiness, the antechamber of Paradise that is the transforming union. But such is human misery that even this favor does not consist, as is popularly believed, in absolute preservation from all sin. The Blessed Virgin is unique in all her privileges, and we can admire this singular gift in her. But the confirmation in grace of which theologians speak consists only in such an abundance of sanctifying grace, with such deep roots in the soul, that the soul remains protected from every serious act that could deprive it of the state of grace. Such a blessing does not include of itself a knowledge of the grace of final perseverance, for according to the Council of Trent no one can have absolute assurance of final perseverance except through a special revelation. Certainly, then, this privilege does not exclude falling into semideliberate faults, a misery we find even in holy souls.

These fundamental principles lead us to a very consoling conclusion: when, over a period of years, we have exercised our good will, have put up a real struggle for virtue, and have tried to combat our defects and avoid falling into sin, the persistence of these defects and of our falls is not of itself a proof that we are going backward. An outward, and to some extent inward, persistence of defects is compatible with a genuine, though hidden, progress.

Wishing to maintain souls in humility and to give them a sort of counterweight to His graces, God permits continued semideliberate falls. He allows defects to continue, at least as to that which is external and more or less involuntary about them, and at times these defects will even appear to have increased. Happy is the individual who in spite of the apparent uselessness of his efforts humbly perseveres! The day will come when by the grace of God he will sing of victory!

What are the positive signs, we may ask, by which someone can know that he is progressing in the way of perfection? Among various ones that might be given, we shall limit ourselves to two that are proofs not only of progress but also of perfection. They are hunger for God and the desire to do His will.

Hunger for God

The appetite of bodily hunger, the need the body feels for food, is a sign of bodily health. So also the hunger for God, the need the soul feels of being filled with Him, is a sign of spiritual health. This hunger is not of itself something sensible. It can be found in states of aridity and desolation and is very marked when the soul is going through what St. John of the Cross calls the "dark night." It may be pleasant and consoling; but it can also be anguish and even torment. Obscure contemplation, which is the beginning of infused contemplation, is nothing but the soul's feeling of emptiness and of a need for God, although the individual himself may not be clearly aware of this. This sense of need for God becomes acute precisely when the soul becomes spiritually disenchanted with creatures, when nothing created can satisfy it and human satisfactions are flat and insipid to it. Disillusioned with creatures and still not consciously enjoying union with God, the individual has the sensation of a great loneliness, of an immense emptiness that has to be filled.

Rule 12

This hunger for God is compatible with our failings if instead of indulging them we sincerely lament and combat them. And it can even exist along with sins of frailty if we quickly repent of them, rise up, and try to make amends. It is a grace of election that prepares the way for that most excellent grace, union with God.

Scripture tells us that God disposes all things sweetly. Before giving grace, He awakens in the soul a desire for it. Desire for grace prepares the soul to receive it, because desire expands the soul and, as it were, enlarges its capacity. "Open thy mouth wide, and I will fill it," says the Lord (Ps. 80:11). "Expand your soul through desire and I will fill it." Desire also prepares for grace inasmuch as a desire supposes the recognition of a need. A person desires only what he does not have. His desire is transformed into a prayer and a plea. Desiring grace, we ask for it; and asking for it we place the condition required for receiving it. "Ask, and it shall be given you" (Matt. 7:7).

But this hunger for God is not just any desire whatsoever. Frequently a hidden desire, it is always an intense and constant one. It takes its origin from the virtue of hope and is perfected through the gift of knowledge. Through hope, the so-often-forgotten virtue, faith is transformed into charity, and supernatural knowledge of God is converted into divine love. Through a living faith we know the lovableness of God. Knowing Him, we desire to possess Him, and this desire is the work of hope. "You would not desire Me, if you did not already possess Me," says Jesus to the soul in the *Imitation*. God crowns this desire with charity, by which we are united to God and possess Him even in this life.

Understanding what God is, we understand by contrast the futility of everything created. Intimately, experimentally feeling the vanity of all that is not God, we empty ourselves and cut ourselves free from every creature. This disillusionment with creatures must not be confused with a mere human disappointment, possibly associated with a kind of unhealthy romanticism. It is a profound inner disenchantment with creatures, the kind that led the wise man to say, after having tasted of all the satisfactions this world has to offer, "Vanity of vanities, and all is vanity" (Eccles. 1:2).

One aspect of this disillusionment with creatures is that keen awareness of the fleetingness of time and the brevity of life so characteristic of those whom God sanctifies quickly and snatches from the world in the flower of youth. Reading the abundant correspondence of St. Thérèse of the Child Jesus, for example, one finds at every step the obbligato theme of the ephemeralness of life and the longing for Heaven. In a letter to Celine she wrote,

> Oh, indeed, it is very hard to live on earth. But tomorrow, within an hour, we shall arrive in port. My God, what shall we see then? What is that life which will have no end? The Lord will be the soul of our soul. Unfathomable mystery! St. Paul will clarify it for us: "The eye of man has not seen the uncreated light, his ear has not heard the incomparable melodies of heaven, and his heart cannot comprehend what it is that is reserved for him in the future life." And all this will come soon, very soon, if we love Jesus with passion!

And in her poem "My Song for Today," there vibrates at once the intimate sense of the brevity of life:

> My life is an instant
> a passing hour,
> my life is a moment
> ephemeral and fleeting.

and the immense desire for the day of eternity:

> When the sun without setting
> shines for my soul,
> on the harp of the angels
> I will sing to the day
> that knows no end.

It is impossible to come to a profound realization that every-thing here below passes without desiring the good that never passes. Nor can we watch the years go by, taking with them so much that is close to us, without longing for the "eternal years" of which the Psalmist speaks. Who does not naturally love the spring, when the trees become green again, the rosebushes bloom, and all of nature is decked with new finery? And who does not long for that other spring that will never end? Again in the words of Thérèse:

> Here below all the lilies die,
> the songs of the birds are short.
> I dream of a spring which will endure
> forever ... forever.

These sublime longings have their cause in hope. They are perfected by the action of the Holy Spirit through the gift of knowledge. As a child weeps over broken toys, so the soul weeps over the things that formerly were the enchantment of life. But its tears are divinely consoled. For in place of these trifles, the fascination for which had kept its true good hidden, the gift of knowledge reveals God to it as its one true sufficiency. "For the bewitching of vanity obscureth good things, and the wandering of concupiscence overturneth the innocent mind" (Wisd. 4:12). The soul understands that he who possesses God lacks nothing. God alone is enough!

So it is that the hunger for God is born in us. Hope becomes something gigantic, creating this hunger and preparing charity, which grows proportionately, uniting the soul to God and nourishing it with God. "He who comes to me shall not hunger, and he who believes in me shall never thirst" (John 6:35; cf. Sir. 24:29). As hunger grows, possession becomes more perfect. The process continues until eternity, when this hunger will be fully satisfied. "Blessed are they who hunger and thirst after justice, for they shall be satisfied" (Matt. 5:6). And what is this process, if not the full progress, growth, and development of the spiritual life?

The Desire to Do the Will of God

Sanctity lies in love. Now, love can be either *affective* or *effective*. Affective love is subject to illusion, especially when the emotions are involved in it. Effective love does not deceive, and it manifests the sincerity of affective love. By affective love we say to God, with words or from the depths of our heart, "I love You." By effective love we carry out God's will. We naturally first of all love God, and tell Him so. But then we reflect, "If I love Him, I ought to please Him, give Him all the pleasure I can, do whatever He wishes. If this calls for sacrifice, so much the better." Now how will I give God pleasure? By doing His will, for He Himself has assured me, "If anyone love me, he will keep my word" (John 14:23). When in order to prove to Him my love I set about to do His will, my love has become effective.

I must remember that the will of God can be fulfilled in various ways. I can submit myself to it solely for fear of punishment, through servile fear. Or again, making a virtue of necessity, I can accept God's will with simple resignation, adopting a "what else can I do?" attitude. Finally, I can fulfill the will of God for the sole motive of pleasing Him. The real sign of progress in the spiritual life is the desire to carry out the will of God in this last way. Rather than speak of a desire to do God's will in this case, we can better speak of "love" for that will.

Perfect love for the will of God is universal. It extends to every manifestation of God's will, whether He commands or merely desires, and includes God's will simply as manifested by the external course of events. Perfect love is also exclusive; by it I love nothing but the will of God. Determined to die to my own will and to my personal desires, I must love everything that God loves, only what God loves, and only because God loves it. In this way, my will comes to be transformed into, and, as it were, fused with the will of God. Here is the essence of holiness, for I am united with God insofar as my will becomes one with His.

Love for the will of God is a trait common to all the saints. Not all have been martyrs or great penitents. Not all have been virgins. Not all have illuminated the world with their doctrine. But each and every one has loved the will of God and fulfilled it to the point of heroism. When love for the will of God has become a real passion absorbing all the energies of the soul, here is the surest sign there is of spiritual maturity. Every saint is the proof.

The Saint of saints is our Lord. And in the Gloria of the Mass, we are assured that He alone deserves to be called "Saint" or holy, "*Tu solus sanctus*—Thou alone art holy." But the characteristic trait of Jesus, the whole perfection of His life, so exalted as to be beyond our comprehension, is summed up in love for the will of the heavenly Father. The first word of Jesus upon entering the world expressed His absorption in the will of His Father: "Behold, I come ... to do thy will, O God" (Heb. 10:7; cf. Ps. 39:8-9). Instead of assigning Him some easy task, His Father's will demanded sacrifice. But Jesus embraced it generously: "He humbled himself, becoming obedient to death, even to death on a cross" (Phil. 2:8).

Jesus had one single preoccupation during His whole life. "My food is to do the will of him who sent me, to accomplish his work" (John 4:34). He was completely given over to His Father's will. "So be it, Father, for thus it has seemed good in Your sight." Above all, He could truthfully say those words that express the pure essence of holiness and the highest perfection: "I do always the things that are pleasing to him" (John 8:29).

The carrying out of His Father's will was by no means always a pure pleasure for our Lord. At times, as during His agony in Gethsemane, victory came only after a terrible struggle between the divine will and the legitimate longings of His human will. But the unfaltering disposition of Jesus is expressed in words uttered during that tremendous struggle: "Not my will but thine be done" (Luke 22:42.) Before dying, Jesus contemplated from the height of His Cross the whole panorama of His life. He looked to see if even one iota of His Father's will had not been carried out. And seeing that everything was completely done, He exclaimed, "It is consummated!" (John 19:30). "The will of my Father has been perfectly fulfilled." Only then did He bow His head and yield up His spirit.

In the face of the example of Christ, it is not to be wondered at that all the saints, especially as they attain the very heights of sanctity, have one desire and one only. They are captivated by a love, a passion, for the will of God.

Rule 13

We must awaken in ourselves an ever-growing hunger for Jesus.

The total surrender of oneself to God is of incalculable importance in all spirituality, and especially in the spirituality of the cross. In our set of rules for the spiritual life, total surrender is the central point; the earlier rules prepare the way for it, and the later rules carry it through.

The substance of Christianity and the essence of perfection lie in charity, which is a mutual love or a love of friendship. Now three acts, or three stages, belong to love. There is the love that is offered, the love that is given, and the love that possesses. Or again, there is the love that desires, the love that hands itself over, and the love that unites. In the first stage, God manifests Himself and the soul desires Him. In the second, God asks and the soul surrenders. In the third, God and the soul mutually possess each other and are united to each other. These three stages correspond respectively to this rule and to the two rules that follow. We shall consider each one.

God disposes all things most sweetly and accommodates Himself admirably to our being and activity. Whenever He wants something from us that of its nature is costly to us, He makes its fulfillment easy by inspiring us with a desire to do it. We readily do what we desire to do, and desire makes a rough road smooth.

Desire dilates the soul, creates in the soul a greater capacity, makes of the soul an enlarged emptiness that God and His graces hurry to fill. "*Dilata os tuum, et implebo illud* – Open thy mouth wide, and I will fill it," says the Lord (Ps. 80:11). According as we desire God more, we possess Him more, especially in the next life but also even in this life.

Desire is highly praised in the Sacred Scriptures, and all true religion before Jesus Christ can be summed up as a gigantic desire for the coming of the Messiah, the Desired One of the Nations. After the coming of Jesus, religion remains an immense desire, the desire for the mystical coming of Jesus to our hearts to fill and possess them; the desire for His last coming, triumphant and glorious, to consummate time and seal eternity.

Love, we have said, is the essence of Christianity and the very model and form of perfection. Now, is not love on earth chiefly an insatiable desire? In Heaven love will be possession, but on earth it is a hunger and thirst that cannot be satisfied. No wonder that love and sorrow are inseparable on earth, opposite sides of one reality. Bishop Gay has said of sorrow that it is "perhaps nothing but another name for love on earth." If love is desire and desire sorrow, love becomes a kind of martyrdom. The more insatiable the desire, so much the more agonizing the martyrdom, as we see in those who achieve the heights of sanctity. The desire to possess God was a martyrdom for the Blessed Virgin, the cause of her death. It moved St. Paul to exclaim that he longed "to depart and to be with Christ" (Phil. 1:23), and St. Teresa to affirm that she died because she did not die.

Small wonder that spiritual authors ascribe such importance to desire in the spiritual life, regarding it as a thermometer or a gauge by which the spiritual life is measured. When a person's desires are sinful, his life is sinful. If his desires are worldly, his life is worldly. If his desires are frivolous, his life is frivolous. If a man has ceased to desire God and divine things, his spiritual life is either dead or dying. If his desires for God are mediocre, his life is lukewarm. When his desire for God is ardent, his life is fervent; when his desire for God is insatiable, his life is perfect and holy.

How a priest is consoled to find himself among souls of great desires, noble ambitions, insatiable longings! These individuals are the timber of which saints and apostles are made, to set fire to the world. On the other hand, how distressing it is to see an individual in whom all desire is extinct, all noble ambition snuffed out, all holy aspiration dead! Disillusioned, spiteful individuals trying to convince themselves that holiness is an illusion! Deadened souls in whom all spiritual resiliency has been extinguished!

But is it really possible to find someone without desires? Disillusioned with creatures. we shall indeed one day desire none of the ephemeral and perishable goods around us. Knowing the inconstancy of human love, we shall close our hearts to all egotistical and mean affections. But how can anyone who knows Jesus, if only slightly, fail to burn with a desire to possess and love Him? The Church sings beautifully of Jesus that He is *"totus desiderabilis* — in every way desirable." Jesus is desirable as God and desirable as man. Jesus is desirable in His greatness and in His weakness; in the glory of His triumphs and in the shame of His sorrows; in the infinite power of His miracles and in the bitterness of His tears; in the whole rich scale of His mysteries, as an infant in Bethlehem, a youth in Nazareth, a miracle worker in Galilee, a martyr in Gethsemane, a victim on Calvary, a host in the Eucharist.

Jesus is desirable in whatever circumstances we find ourselves, for there is no desire of the human heart that is not satisfied in

Him. If we are sad and desire some taste of joy to sweeten the cup of bitterness, we have Jesus, the joy of Heaven who has become our joy on earth. Jesus consoles us as He consoled the apostles in the sadness of His departure from them, assuring them, "But I will see you again, and your heart shall rejoice, and your joy no one shall take from you" (John 16:22). "Abide in my love ... that my joy may be in you, and that your joy may be made full' (John 15:10-11). If we are tired out by our trip along the rough road of life and our hearts are seeking rest, where will we find that rest except with the beloved disciple on the bosom of our Savior? Jesus invites us to follow Him and imitate Him precisely in order that we may find rest for our souls (see Matt. 11:29). Opening His arms and His heart, He invites us, "Come to me, all you who labor and are burdened, and I will give you rest" (Matt. 11:28). You who are tired out from work and suffering, come to Me and I will be your rest and your consolation.

Are we in search of a stable and enduring peace to calm our restlessness and pacify our troubled spirit? In Jesus and only in Jesus can we find it. For He and only He could say in truth, "Peace I leave with you, my peace I give to you" (John 14:27). I do not give the false and deceiving peace of the world; I give my peace, a peace that gives rest in time and in eternity. I give that peace that "surpasses all understanding" (Phil. 4:7), that causes "peace to reign in your hearts" (see Col. 3:15) and joy to overflow in them. Jesus the joy of Heaven is also the peace of earth. "For he himself is our peace" (Eph. 2:14), says St. Paul. He has reconciled earth with Heaven and men with God, establishing in us that reign that is "peace and joy in the Holy Spirit" (Rom. 14:17).

Are we passing through the supreme trial of life, interior desolation of soul? Do we seem to have no one to love, and does it seem that there is no one who loves us? Do we seem abandoned in the midst of the selfishness of men? Well, in spite of all, Jesus has remained with us, a most faithful friend and companion. St. Peter's overhasty claim (Mark 14:31) belongs most truly on the lips of Jesus, for though all should abandon us, He never will. "And behold, I am with you all days, even unto the consummation of the world" (Matt. 28:20).

When our mind is seeking out the truth, where shall it find truth if not in Jesus "the light of the world" (John 8:12), Jesus who is truth itself? To whom else shall we go to avoid deception if He alone has the words of everlasting life (see John 6:69)? The words of men are deceitful and dead words; the words of God, though communicated to the soul without a sound, are words of truth and life.

When health is gone and strength has ebbed with the years, when we feel that life is getting away from us, and the coldness and the solitude of the grave lie open at our feet, how there reawakens in our soul the longing for immortality, for a life that does not end, crumble, and die! Well, Jesus has told us, "I am the life" (see John 14:6). "I came that they may have life, and have it more abundantly" (John 10:10). "I am the bread of life" (John 6:35). The gift of Jesus in the Eucharist sows in the furrows of our souls the seed of immortality. "If anyone eat of this bread he shall live forever" (John 6:52). "He who believes in me, even if he die, shall live" (John 11:25).

If we have the souls of artists and long for a beauty that does not wither or fade, an ideal and absolute beauty, where shall we find the beauty for which we long but in Him who has been called the most beautiful of the sons of men (see Ps. 44:3)? And if above all we want a friend, a friend who will satisfy the imperious and irresistible need of the human heart, a faithful friend who will never betray us—who is that friend if not Jesus, who, as Scripture says, "is called Faithful and True" (Rev. 19:11)? There is not one single need of the human heart that is not satisfied in Jesus. He is truly "wholly desirable," desirable in every way. How could anyone possibly not desire Him?

What does it mean "to desire Jesus"? First of all, it means to desire Heaven, for Heaven is the full possession of Jesus. The truth is that we do not desire Heaven enough. With our attachments to the goods of this world, we are very different from the Christians of the first ages of Christianity. Christian life in those days was dominated by the longing for the coming of Jesus. Christians greeted one another with the Hebrew word "*Maranatha*—Come, Lord Jesus." Almost obsessed by the shortness of life, they had constantly before their eyes the truth that soon the day of liberty would come, and the soul, free of the bonds of the mortal body, would go forth to the full possession of its Lord. The first ages of Christianity were still fragrant with the mortal presence of Jesus in the world. Who could have lived with Jesus once without loving Him and longing to be with Him again?

His apostles so loved Him that they were overwhelmed with sorrow when He told them He must leave them. "Let not your heart be troubled," He said to them. "You believe in God, believe also in me" (John 14:1). "A little while and you shall see me no longer; and again a little while and you shall see me" (John 16:16). It is true that in a little while you will not see me, but have confidence, wait patiently, and again, in a little while, you will see me. The first Christians found their comfort in that "little while" of which Jesus spoke. The whole of the present life, they knew, is but a little while. When Jesus ascended into Heaven, the disciples could not take their eyes off the sky into which their Master had disappeared. "How can it be possible that we are not to see Him again?" And then they recalled His own words, "In a little while you will see me again." Those words gave them strength to tear themselves away and return to the struggle and toil of the world, to persecution and martyrdom.

If we loved Jesus, we should desire the day of our death as the day of the termination of our exile, the day in which we too will see Him whom we have so loved: "A little while, and you will see me." Desiring Heaven more, we should love the earth less.

To desire Jesus is not only to desire Heaven; it is to desire an increase of grace in our souls. For grace is nothing else but the life of Jesus in us. The seed of glory, of blessedness, and of Heaven, grace has its source in the very heart of Christ. From there, as from a filled-up fountain, it overflows to us. It gradually works its way into us, transforming us and making us more and more like God. Holiness is nothing else but the perfect divinization of the soul. When we shall have become impregnated with the grace of Christ and our whole heart filled up with Him, then we shall be saints. Each shall be able to say with St. Paul, "It is now no longer I that live, but Christ lives in me" (Gal. 2:20).

To desire Jesus is to desire not only grace but all the means that will develop it in us. Among these means, there is one that includes all the others. This is the cross. Yes, the cross in its many manifestations. Jesus came to us by the way of the cross, and we cannot go to Him except by way of the cross. To go to Jesus is to go not through glory but through humiliation; not by way of convenience but by way of renunciation; not by way of self-seeking but by way of abnegation; not by way of pleasure but by way of mortification. In a word, we go to Jesus by dying to ourselves. Jesus longed for

His Passion. "I have a baptism to be baptized with [a baptism of blood], and how distressed I am until it is accomplished!" (Luke 12:50). He desired to suffer as a means of gaining our souls and bringing them to union with Him.

To unite ourselves to Christ, we, too, must desire to suffer. Yet, although there is no other way, how many of us there are who take scandal at the cross like St. Peter. When Jesus told His apostles that He was going to suffer, Peter protested, "This will never happen to thee" (Matt. 16:22). The cross is very beautiful in theory; but when it actually presents itself, how few receive it well! With many, the desire for Jesus is purely theoretical and idealistic. It must in fact become a threefold practical desire: the desire for Heaven, or the full possession of God; the desire for sanctifying grace and its increase, or the highest possession of God available to us on earth; the desire for the indispensable means to the growth of grace, the cross. "Blessed are they who hunger and thirst for justice, for they shall be satisfied" with the fullness of God (Matt. 5:6).

Rule 14

Having duly prepared ourselves, we must formally make our total surrender to God.

Expressly, the total surrender is an act by which a person freely, and with complete awareness of what he is doing, offers himself to God in order that the will of God may be perfectly accomplished in him. Though formally an act, this surrender produces a state or habitual disposition through which the individual remains constantly offered and surrendered to God. Religious profession is one type of total surrender. It is an act, the act of making religious vows; but by those very vows a person is established in a permanent and definitive state.

Very closely connected with the total surrender is the notion of "spiritual sacrifice." Sacrifice involves essentially two acts, one divine and the other human. In the human act, the victim offers himself to God, gives himself over to the divine will, to be immolated. This human act can be called the offertory. The divine act, or consecration, is the act by which God accepts the victim and in this way consecrates it. This is the consecration.

Any contract of donation is completed only when these two acts are united: the donor's act of offering the gift and the recipient's act of accepting it. Once the recipient accepts, the gift is his and belongs to him in full right. Now, sacrifice is like a solemn contract of donation between God and man. Man offers, hands over, the gift of himself. When God accepts the gift, the individual is no longer his own and belongs completely to God. He is consecrated to God, because whatever is dedicated to divine service is said to be consecrated. The total surrender is of key importance in the spirituality of the cross precisely because this spirituality has sacrifice at its very core. Sacrifice is a solemn giving to God. Man's role is to offer and surrender himself, to hand himself over, not by halves or with limitations but totally and without qualification, as God deserves.

The state produced by the act of total giving is the source of what has been called the chain of love. The chain of love is formed by those who strive to live offered and surrendered to the will of God, immolated and sacrificed. They cannot be alone, however, for when they are alone, their oblation is worth nothing. They must be in union with the Word. Jesus Christ and His Blessed Mother are the supreme examples of the total surrender, the two perfect illustrations of this habitual disposition that plays a part in the chain of love.

The first act of the Word upon becoming man was to give Himself over completely and totally to the will of His Father. What His Father asked of Him was a whole life of sacrifice and immolation. St. Paul tells us that on entering the world Jesus said, "Behold, I come … to do thy will, O God" (Heb. 10:7). The Blessed Virgin, too, began her mission as co-redemptrix of the human race, the mediatrix of all graces and Mother of God and men, by offering herself without restriction to the will of God. "Behold the handmaid of the Lord; be it done to me according to thy word" (Luke 1:38). The life of any saint would tell the same story could we but know his intimate relations with God.

Rule 14

Each new stage, each new ascent, in the spiritual life is marked by a distinct act of total surrender, especially beginning with the illuminative way. In the economy of our justification God has imposed on Himself the rule of not carrying out any of His intimate operations within us without first asking our consent. These mysterious operations either are themselves a true sacrifice or they require one. Since God wants the sacrifice to be free and voluntary, He never sacrifices us unless we freely offer ourselves to be sacrificed.

The heavenly Father sacrificed His Son, Jesus Christ, only because Jesus offered Himself voluntarily, as Isaiah had foretold: "He was offered because it was His own will" (Isa. 53:7). Our Lord affirmed it of Himself: "For this reason the Father loves me, because I lay down my life that I may take it up again. No one takes it from me, but I lay it down of myself. I have the power to lay it down, and I have the power to take it up again" (John 10:17–18). Likewise, when God desired the Blessed Virgin to cooperate in the work of the Redemption and sacrifice herself in union with her Son, He sent an angel to ask her consent. The work of redemption did not begin until Mary said, "Behold the handmaid of the Lord" (Luke 1:38).

How are we to know when God is asking some special sacrifice of us? And if we do not know, how can we possibly make our act of acceptance beforehand? Precisely because we do not know the special sacrifice that God may ask of us. He inspires us to a total surrender. Such a surrender includes whatever God may ask.

To be efficacious and not merely verbal, to have true dignity and seriousness, total giving must be preceded by total self-renunciation.

We can never give without losing ownership of what we give. To give is to renounce ownership. Since we are giving our very selves, since we ourselves are being offered and handed over, the giving plainly cannot take place unless we truly renounce ourselves. Total giving and total self-renunciation are not two distinct realities, but one reality under a negative and positive aspect. Self-giving is the positive aspect, self-renunciation the negative. To give ourselves, we must dispossess ourselves of ourselves. If the renunciation is not total, the surrender or handing over will not be total.

Renunciation or abnegation is in a certain way total by its very nature. Self-denial, the negation of ourselves and of our disordered inclinations, necessarily has something absolute about it. One cannot deny by halves; a thing either is or is not. Self-renunciation can be compared with death, for it is a kind of death in the spiritual order. Nobody can be dead and alive at the same time, or partly dead and partly alive. Like death, real self-renunciation must be total.

There is one more reason why total surrender demands total renunciation. As a vase cannot be completely filled with perfume unless it is completely emptied of everything else, so our soul cannot be completely filled with God unless it is empty of all that is not God. Now, in the last analysis, the reason for the total surrender is not and cannot be any other than to attain full union with God. But God can fill a soul only when through complete renunciation it has become completely empty.

To be united with God, we must be elevated and lifted up. Every earthly tie must be broken. One bond only, however insignificant, will suffice to hold us. A bird cannot fly freely, whether it be imprisoned in a steel cage or held only by a thread of silk. Renunciation breaks the ties that hold us and permits us to rise to God. If one cord remains uncut, our renunciation is not total and we remain fastened to the earth. Renunciation must be definitive and perpetual—it is forever. When we hand over something only for a determined time, we are not said to give it but to lend it. Now, the total surrender as a complete and perfect giving must be definitive and perpetual, not a loan. The corresponding self-renunciation or dispossession of self must be just as definitive and perpetual. We give ourselves exactly in the measure in which we cease to belong to ourselves.

No wonder that true total surrender is so difficult and so laborious! How easily we can deceive ourselves, imagining that we have really made the total surrender because in a moment of passing enthusiasm we pronounce the formula that expresses total surrender. The truth is that as long as there is no total renunciation of self, total surrender is an illusion. On the other hand, when we have truly renounced ourselves, our surrender is genuine and effective.

Every virtue has a part to play in the total surrender. Inordinate inclinations of our sense appetite would make impossible our surrender to God. The virtue of temperance represses these appetites. The virtue of fortitude gives us the constancy to make our renunciation total and enduring. Prudence moderates excesses in the application of the renunciation and guides us to make the dispossession with due discretion. As for justice, there is no greater justice than to give back to God what is God's; He is Lord and Sovereign of all that we are and have.

The theological virtues enter in even more actively. Faith makes us see the incomparable spiritual advantages that our sacrifice brings and the right God has to receive it. Hope, already exercised in the desire to belong to God, now animates us to give ourselves over to Him, for we know that the secret of our true happiness lies in surrender to Him. Total surrender is, above all, the specific and supreme act of charity. The initial act of love is the desire to possess God. "You would not desire to love Me, if you did not already love Me," Jesus says in the *Imitation*. But true love not only desires to give, its very essence is to give. We give not only what we have but above all what we are. To love is to give, and especially to give oneself. The supreme love on all the earth is the love that brings to completion the absolute giving of ourselves to God—the total surrender.

Once more, we are confronted with the essence of the spirit of the cross: love and sorrow. Total surrender is sorrow because it is a sacrifice; it is love because it is giving. Sorrow is the essence of the total surrender. Love is its cause and its goal. We surrender ourselves because we love and in order to consummate our love in union.

Because the total surrender is so basic, it cannot be confined to the spirituality of the cross or to any other particular school. It is present in all true spirituality, sometimes under another name, sometimes with different variations and modalities.

Ignatian spirituality finds its most famous expression in that wonderful little work *The Spiritual Exercises*. On the very first page, St. Ignatius tells us that a man must be "indifferent" with respect to everything created. What is this indifference but an attitude of detachment and total self-renunciation? Now, total renunciation of self, as we have already seen, is but the negative aspect of "total surrender." This is why commentators on the *Exercises* teach that this indifference is not apathetic, passive, or quietist but eminently active and operative; it detaches a man from creatures only in order that he may fly to God, surrender himself to God, and be united with Him.

At the end of the *Exercises* is a section called "Contemplation as a means to love." A sort of summary of the *Exercises* and a compendium of the whole of Christian perfection, it concludes with a true "total surrender" expressed in the beautiful, traditional formula: "Take, O Lord, my entire liberty, my memory, my understanding, and my will. All that I am and have, Thou hast given me, and I surrender it all to Thee, to be so disposed as accords with Thy divine will. Give me Thy love and grace, and with these I am rich enough; I desire nothing more."

Another of the most celebrated spiritualities in the Church is that of the so-called French school, Berullian or Sulpician spirituality. It was adopted by the religious families of Cardinal Berulle (Oratorians), Fr. Olier (Sulpicians), St. John Eudes (Eudists and Religious of the Good Shepherd), St. Vincent de Paul (Vincentians and Sisters of Charity), St. Louis Grignion de Montfort (Company of Mary and Daughters of Wisdom), Ven. Libermann, and others. Of great influence in the spiritual formation of a large number of the clergy in our seminaries, it is represented by such men as Bossuet, Thomassin, Msgr. Gay, and Fr. Faber.

This spirituality looks first to the primordial duty of every man not only as a Christian but simply as God's rational creature, to adore God. Jesus Christ came into the world precisely with the mission, intimately united to that of His priesthood, to raise up true adorers who would adore the Father in spirit and in truth. "God is spirit, and they who worship him must worship in spirit and in truth" (John 4:24). This means that men must adore in union with the Word, Eternal Truth, and under the motion of the Holy Spirit, Spirit of the Father and the Son. The proper role of the incarnate Word is to be the mediator of redemption and adoration through His sacrifice. No one can carry out the great duty of adoration or succeed in being a perfect adorer of the Godhead except by participating in the "states" of the divine Mediator and perfect Adorer. We must unite ourselves to Christ, transform ourselves into Him, thinking, willing, and working with Him for the glory of the Father. Such union with Christ is realized by means of "renunciation" and "adherence." We renounce ourselves and adhere to Jesus Christ. We dispossess ourselves and enter into communion with the "states" of the incarnate Word.

Fr. Olier contrasts quite clearly the individual who has renounced himself and the individual who has not. He who is not yet dispossessed is self-centered. Literally full of self, he confides and trusts in himself and desires to be esteemed by others. Habitually agitated, disturbed, restless, sad, ill-humored, he takes affront at the slightest word or least discourtesy. On the other hand, a man who has renounced himself is a man who has gone out of himself and is completely empty of self. Distrusting his own powers and relying on Jesus Christ, he is forgetful of self and tries to hide himself. He always maintains an even disposition, lives in peace, and permits nothing to irritate him. He suffers all things without disturbance of soul.

Now, is not Fr. Olier describing the very total self-renunciation of which we were speaking earlier? Is not "adherence" to Jesus Christ or communion with the "states" of the incarnate Word simply the positive element of the total surrender? By this adherence we first of all give joyful ratification to the supernatural state in which we in fact find ourselves. We accept all that God has disposed for us and everything that Christ has done for us. In addition, we enter into the spirit of each one of our Lord's mysteries. While these mysteries may indeed have passed as far as the circumstances of time are concerned, in their power they *are* present and enduring. The love Jesus put into these mysteries remains, and the dispositions He had in the past He continues to have now in His divine heart. Communion in the life of Christ requires a mutual donation. The very name indicates this — communion, "mutual union." "It is called communion," says Fr. Olier, "because the soul gives itself to God in order to share in His gifts." A person dispossesses himself only for the purpose of belonging to Jesus Christ. The spirituality of Berulle and Olier is, then, a special form of the "total surrender."

Moreover, the celebrated "true devotion" to Mary as taught by St. Grignion de Montfort is nothing but a total surrender, a consecration of all that we are and have to the incarnate Wisdom through Mary.

Franciscan spirituality has perhaps been more popularized among the faithful than any other, thanks to the third order extended throughout the world. This spirituality has two fundamental notes: poverty and seraphic love. Poverty makes itself effective by the privation of material goods insofar as this is prudent. But poverty is above all affective, a total detachment of self from creatures. This detachment from everything created is taken to be the necessary condition that God may become our single treasure, our only wealth, our one love. The celebrated exclamation of St. Francis expresses this well: "My God and my all!" "For me, nothing counts but God," he would say. "God is all, everything else nothing." St. Francis's words are a reminder of St. Paul speaking of the blessed state of creation when time will have come to an end: "That God may be all in all" (1 Cor. 15:28). Do we not see here the two aspects, negative and positive, of the total surrender, a poverty that despoils us of everything in order to give us over totally to the love of Christ?

A study of other Catholic schools of spirituality would show that in one form or another the "total surrender" is an essential element in Christian perfection. The proper character of the total surrender in the spirituality of the cross lies in the aspect of sacrifice. The efficient and final cause of the surrender is love; its essence, sorrow; its condition, purity. Purity is the necessary condition because the victim cannot be accepted if it is not pure. The sacrifice must be united to that of Jesus Christ, and no one can be united to Him unpurified. Purity, in its negative aspect, is not really distinct from total renunciation of self. In the spirituality of the cross, the three characteristics of the total surrender are then love, sorrow, and purity.

Rule 15

Having formally made over everything to God, we must put this commitment into practice, actually giving to our Savior each thought and word and work.

Through the "total surrender" we give ourselves to God in principle and by right. When we do this sincerely and with our whole will, we have already done a great deal; we have laid the foundation of all the rest. Nevertheless, the task is still before us of making the surrender effective. What we have given in general we must now give in utmost detail. What we have handed over by right we must now hand over in fact. What belongs to God by an act of our will must now become His by the activity of all our powers.

God as our Creator has the most absolute right over us. As His creatures, we belong to Him wholly and completely. But because God willed man to be the free master of his own activities, man is expected by the free determination of his will to surrender himself to God by a new title. In the state of original justice, man was God's in this way. But sin, original and actual, repudiated and annulled man's original donation. Jesus Christ then redeemed us, restoring to us the power to give ourselves to God through that free and loving surrender that is the fruit of charity. Already belonging to God through creation, we can offer ourselves anew to God through charity, give ourselves freely and lovingly. When we say to God, "I love You," we signify that we esteem God above all things, that we prefer Him to everything else, that we desire for Him every good.

But we further signify that we surrender ourselves to Him, give ourselves to Him with all that we are, do, and have.

The practical way to make our surrender effective is to consecrate to God our activity. A mother manifests her love for her child not only by caresses and words of endearment but also by consecrating herself to his service; she literally squanders on him her time, her strength, her health, her life.

This is how we must give ourselves to God. We must aim to carry out His will completely, satisfy His every desire, accept whatever He disposes, comply with His every wish. Total surrender demands of us that we consecrate ourselves to God's service for the perfect accomplishment of His will. The way to serve another human being is to do as he wishes, sacrificing our own will and fulfilling his. This also is how we serve God.

Now, the divine will manifests itself chiefly in three ways: the will that commands, the will that disposes, the will that counsels or desires.

The will that commands is a manifestation of God's sovereign authority. God has employed it immediately in the commandments, mediately in the precepts of the Church. By this will, God commands that this thing be done and that avoided. Not to subject oneself to this will, or to disobey it, is to commit a sin, serious or light, according to the importance of the precept.

The will that disposes is manifested by means of events, favorable or adverse. These events may come from irrational nature, or they may come immediately from the free will of men. In any case, they come under at least the permissive will of God, for nothing, great or small, takes place in the whole universe without God at least permitting it. The fall of an empire or the fall of a hair—God's plan has a place for both.

The will that counsels is manifested not when God commands or disposes but simply when He makes known a desire, a wish. To fail to satisfy this divine will is an imperfection, not a sin. Priestly, religious, or other vocations pertain to this will, as do also the inspirations of the Holy Spirit and all the motions of grace that incline us to practice the virtues.

Corresponding to the three manifestations of the divine will, there are three degrees in which we may surrender ourselves to it. The first consists in striving to fulfill with increasing fidelity the preceptive will of God, obeying the divine commandments, honoring the precepts of the Church, subjecting ourselves to the orders of our lawful superiors, and carrying out the obligations of our state. This solid, necessary foundation for the whole spiritual edifice admits of no substitute. Without it, we build on sand. It is the first purification of the soul and corresponds to the purgative way. This surrender requires us to eliminate not only mortal sin but also that habitual venial sin that is so contrary to a fervent spiritual life. It calls for ceaseless struggle against all deliberate sin, including sins of frailty. Fidelity to God's will here may mean that we eventually receive from God the grace of avoiding even semideliberate venial sins, a misery that oppresses those far advanced in the way of perfection.

The second degree of surrender to God's will consists in applying ourselves to accept ever more readily the will of God as manifested in events, great or small, especially when they are contrary to our plans or when they humiliate or injure us, as do poverty, sickness, failure, loneliness, and interior aridity. The first step here is that resignation to which the most elementary Christian sense counsels us. If the will of God has to be fulfilled regardless, what do we gain by rebelling against it? We only lose our peace of mind and increase our pain. "To kick against the goad" (Acts 9:5) is of no use and only makes things worse.

Resignation, then, is the beginning, but it is insufficient for one who would surrender himself to God completely. We must rise higher and learn to accept joyfully whatever the divine will brings. After all, our faith teaches us that God disposes or permits nothing that is not for our greater good. God is not so much a master who punishes as a Father who loves. Because He loves us, He heals us and purifies us, working to perfect us with the chisel of sorrow.

But even joyful acceptance is not sufficient. We must aim at complete conformity of our will with the will of God by complete abandonment to this same most holy will. But since abandonment responds to the divine will in its every manifestation, it belongs rather to the third stage that we are about to consider.

The third and last degree of surrender to God's will requires us not only to obey the will that commands and accept the will that disposes but to acquiesce completely in the divine good pleasure, knowing that whatever God desires must be holy and sanctifying. To obey the will that commands and accept the will that disposes is the work of justice. But to conform ourselves to the divine will in even its slightest desires; to abandon ourselves to that will in its every manifestation; to wish nothing except what God wishes; to desire nothing except what God desires; to love only what God loves; to die to all self-will in order to live only for the divine will—this is the supreme work of love.

"The sweet, full, living ineffable act of abandonment!" writes Bishop Gay,

Is it not, in fact, the most natural inclination, the most personal and therefore most imperious necessity, in fine, the supreme and decisive act of love? To abandon oneself is more than to give oneself. Jesus gave Himself to us in the Incarnation. But He abandoned Himself to us in His Passion. And He remains abandoned to us in the Eucharist. For this reason the cross and the altar—which at bottom are two aspects of the same thing—the cross and the altar are the last word of the love of Jesus.

To abandon oneself is to renounce oneself, to leave oneself, to dispossess oneself, to lose oneself, without reserve, without missing that which one gives.... To abandon oneself is, as it were, to melt and become liquid, according to the words of the Spouse in the Canticle: "My soul melted when he spoke" (Cant. 5:6). Of itself a liquid has no shape whatever. Its shape is the shape of the vase which contains it. If we put it in ten different sorts of vases it takes on ten different shapes.... So the soul which has abandoned itself to God is liquid under His word. And not only under the word which commands but also under the word of simple desire and of slightest preference.

Abandonment, as St. Francis de Sales explains, is the death of self-will:

We call death a transition in order to signify that death is nothing but a passing from one life to another, and that to die is nothing but to pass beyond the confines of this mortal life in order to arrive at eternal life. To be sure, our will cannot die, just as the soul cannot; but at times it passes beyond the limits of ordinary life to live only by the will of God. And this happens when it does not know of anything, or desire anything, except total abandonment to the good pleasure of divine providence, joining itself in such a way to this good pleasure, that it can be seen no longer, completely hidden as it is with Jesus Christ in God, where it lives, now not it, but the will of God in it.

Bossuet speaks of seeking "something in man that will be perfectly one; an act which will embrace everything in its unity, containing on the one hand everything that there is in man, and on the other hand responding to everything that there is in God." Bossuet finds what he is seeking in the act of abandonment. To abandon oneself is to give oneself wholly, for abandonment is "total surrender," the perfect immolation, the holocaust of the whole man. Abandonment is the sacrifice of the will, and by one's will one gives one's whole self. With true abandonment to God, there remains nothing more that man can give, nothing more that God can ask.

This third stage of surrender implies a special docility to the inspirations of the Holy Spirit. These inspirations become increasingly frequent. If our correspondence grows proportionately, the activity of our spiritual life will be made perfect. The Holy Spirit will take more and more into His own hands our spiritual guidance. The gifts of the Holy Spirit will be exercised with increasing frequency until they come to predominate in our spiritual life.

The predominance of the gifts of the Holy Spirit is the characteristic sign of entry into the mystical life. Under the influence of the gifts, the soul continues to practice the virtues but now in the divine manner proper to the gifts rather than in the human way proper to the simple virtues. In the manner of working proper to man, the human manner, an individual practices the virtues guided and directed by the light of reason, which God has given for this purpose. This is the ascetical period of the spiritual life. Even though we speak of the "human way" here, grace, far from being excluded, is everywhere present. Sanctifying grace transforms the soul, the infused virtues supernaturalize its faculties, actual graces move the faculties in their operations. But in spite of the presence of grace, the manner of acting is still human; for man acts as man so long as his actions have right reason as their rule.

Practiced in this human way, to how many imperfections the virtues are subject! As Scripture says, "The thoughts of mortal men are fearful, and our counsels uncertain" (Wisd. 9:14). How much ignorance there is to obscure reason, how many doubts to torment it, how many limitations to hem it in! Human reason, even illuminated by faith, is like a man feeling his way in the midst of the half darkness of the night.

But when the gifts come to predominate, the Holy Spirit is the one who immediately moves, guides, directs. He indeed causes the practice of the virtues. But now, in this divine manner of operation, the norm of the virtues is not human reason but divine wisdom. What a difference! The virtues do not now suffer from the vacillations, the timidity, the uncertainty of poor human reason. On the contrary, they share in the certainty, the clarity, the immutability of divine reason. Instead of the vacillations of human prudence, there is the audaciousness of the gift of counsel. The inconstancies of a love that is just budding are replaced by the fidelity and fearlessness of heroic love!

Virtues, exercised under the influence of the gifts, are called by St. Thomas "*iam purgati animi* – of the soul already purified" (ST I-II, q. 61, art. 5). They are the virtues of the perfect, the virtues that produce heroic acts and lead to that "heroicity of virtue" that marks the saints. An individual living habitually under the influence of the gifts and moved as constantly by the Holy Spirit as is possible in this life, has by this very fact become godlike not only in his being but in the whole of his activity. He has become as perfectly supernaturalized as he can become on earth. He has surrendered totally to God. There remains only Heaven, where the soul will lose itself forever in the bosom of God—the consummation of the total surrender.

Small wonder that the total surrender is the center, the substance, the essence of the spirituality of the cross! The whole program of the spiritual life can be reduced to three steps: (1) to prepare for the total surrender; (2) to make the surrender explicitly and formally; (3) to complete the surrender by giving to God in each moment of life the whole of one's being and the whole of one's activity.

Rule 16

Surrendered to the divine will, we are to live in spiritual joy and perfect peace.

All love, but especially divine love, tends to the possession of and union with the beloved. This is the law of love, its essence, its life. Love attains its definitive consummation and ultimate perfection, its rest and peace, only when union is realized and possession achieved. So long as it has not arrived at possession, love is desire and hope. But when perfect and consummated, it is a possession that is everlasting—a definitive, eternal union.

Now, union and possession produce in the soul an indescribable inner satisfaction, difficult to define, which is at once exultation, jubilation, satiety, rest, fruition, and happiness. This happiness is the ripest fruit of the Holy Spirit, the Spirit of love. Sacred Scripture calls it "joy in the Holy Spirit." We may call it here "spiritual joy." Considered in all its perfection, this joy is not and cannot be of the earth. For the indefectible union of the soul with God, His definitive possession, is the way of Heaven. Love on earth has to be hope or desire. In the measure in which love increases on earth, it becomes a true martyrdom as hope is enlivened and excruciating desire enkindled.

Yet the love of God on earth is also a fountain of joy. Charity on earth and charity in Heaven are not two charities; they are essentially and substantially one identical love. If in Heaven charity unites us with God and causes us to possess Him, then already on earth it must in some way unite us to Him and cause us to enter into the possession of Him. If faith is the substance of the things for which we hope, and if hope gives us a divine guarantee of possessing these things, charity actually gives us the possession of God and unites us with Him. St. John says, "He who abides in love abides in God, and God in him" (1 John 4:16).

Through charity, the Christian begins to enjoy God now, as a kind of anticipation of Heaven and foretaste of blessedness. If this present delight is not the definitive and consummated happiness of Heaven, neither is it the ephemeral and passing happiness of earth. It is a marvelous mixture of joy and desire, hope and possession, happiness and sorrow. Desire can be a torment. Because the joy that accompanies charity in this life includes desire, it does not exclude sorrow and it coexists with suffering. When Lacordaire asserted that "melancholy is the atmosphere of great souls," perhaps he had in mind the souls of the saints, which carry an ocean of joy in an abyss of sorrow. The saints say with the Psalmist: "According to the multitude of my sorrows in my heart, thy comforts have given joy to my soul" (Ps. 93:19).

The solid foundation, indestructible base, and inexhaustible source of Christian joy is charity. In the measure in which I love God and God loves me, joy will flood my soul. In Baptism I was justified; I received sanctifying grace, with the infused virtues and the gifts of the Holy Spirit, and consequently I received charity. If since Baptism I have had the misfortune to lose charity, contrition and the Sacrament of Penance have given it back to me. The other sacraments worthily received and all the meritorious acts of my life can only have served to increase it. Now, charity, as a love of friendship between God and the soul, supposes two great truths: God loves me; I love God. In this "loves me" and this "*I* love," I must understand that the reference is not just to humanity in general but also quite directly to me.

I Love God

To have absolute certitude that I love God with the supernatural love of charity, I should need a revelation. But human life ordinarily requires no such absolute certitude. For much of human life moral certitude suffices. I have a moral certitude as to who are my parents, who are my brothers, who are the lawfully constituted civil authorities. I have the same moral certitude that I have been baptized, that Fr. John is a real priest, that Eugenio Pacelli is the pope.[4] I have this certitude that a given particular host is consecrated. Such moral certitude is sufficient to put my mind at rest, to give a solid foundation to domestic and social relations and even supernatural ones.

Now God has established the means for me to attain grace and to possess charity. As He has accommodated these means to human weakness, they do not require talent, learning, wealth, or influence; good will suffices. If with good will I make use of the proper means—for example, sacramental Confession—I can have moral certainty of possessing God's grace, and consequently that "the charity of God is poured forth in our hearts by the Holy Spirit who has been given to us" (Rom. 5:5). I ought, then, to lay aside pessimism and scruples and permit the Holy Spirit to give testimony to my spirit that I am of the sons of God (Rom. 8:16) and that consequently I love God with that spontaneous love that

---

[4] Eugenio Pacelli reigned as Pope Pius XII from 1939-1958. —Ed.

a son has for his father. Can a son reasonably doubt that he loves his father? Neither should I doubt that I love God.

Sacred Scripture gives me signs by which I am able to verify my love for God. First of all, is it not the mark of a truly religious person to strive to avoid sin precisely as offensive to God? Does not one who is truly religious wish never to have transgressed the divine precepts? Does he not try to carry them out as far as frailty permits? If he does fall, is it not more through weakness than malice? Jesus said, "If you love me, keep my commandments" (John 14:15).

Another proof that I love God can be found in my readiness to sacrifice myself for Him. He has said, "If anyone wishes to come after me, let him deny himself, and take up his cross, and follow me" (Matt. 16:24). To follow Jesus is the proper movement of love, and to follow Jesus is to embrace suffering. If I embrace Christian suffering, this is a proof that I am following my Savior. No one can love without becoming like the person loved. If I carry in my flesh the marks of the Passion or bear in my soul the ignominies of the Crucified, I am becoming like Him. This is a proof of love for Him. The *Imitation* remarks that one cannot live with love and yet be without sorrow. Surely I can conclude that if I live in sorrow because of God, I do it for the love of God.

Objections may needlessly trouble the sincere Christian about his standing with God. The text of Sacred Scripture is sometimes alleged: "And yet man knoweth not whether he be worthy of love, or hatred" (Eccles. 9:1). But this text does not mean that no one actually knows whether God loves or hates him. It refers rather to our lack of certainty about the future and to the mysterious conduct of God with the good and evil alike. Translated literally from the original Hebrew, it would read, "Man is ignorant of both love and hate." According to the characteristics of Eastern style, by love is to be understood works of love; and by hate, works of the contrary sort. The Scripture is saying that man does not know if the happenings of life, whether favorable or adverse, are rewards or punishments.

It happens frequently that things go ill with the good, as if they were bad, and well with the bad, as if they were good. God is patient with sinners and postpones their punishment, hoping for their conversion. On the other hand, He may try the just, sometimes through the whole of life, in order that they may be more abundantly rewarded in Heaven. Moreover, there are many natural and social calamities — earthquakes, wars, accidents — that come upon all alike, the good and the bad without distinction. God's conduct in the governance of the world is mysterious and beyond our understanding. But we do know that in the end good (love) will definitely triumph, and evil (hate) will be vanquished. And at all events, the above text from Scripture is wrongly quoted as meaning that we have no assurance whatsoever of how we stand in the eyes of God.

Sometimes the words of our Lord are cited: "Many are called, but few are chosen" (Matt. 22:14). Our Lord is understood to be saying that the number of the saved is very few. But here again there is an error in interpretation. Jesus speaks these words on the occasion of the parable of the marriage banquet and applies them to the call to faith, or to the call God makes to all men to come into the Church. This invitation He made first to the Jewish people by means of the prophets. But they despised the invitation and failed to come to the banquet — that is, they made themselves unworthy of the gift of faith. Afterward, by means of the apostles and their successors, God invited the gentiles or all the non-Jewish peoples on earth to enter the Church. The man without the wedding garment represents a person who has faith but not sanctifying grace. Since nobody can enter Heaven without sanctifying grace, while one can indeed belong to the Church without it, this detail confirms the point that the parable is speaking not of salvation but of the call to the Faith.

"Many are called but few are chosen." How can these words be applied to salvation, or how can one argue from them that the number of those to be saved is small, when the parable ends by speaking of the hall as filled with the multitude of those invited to the feast, and when of this multitude only one is thrown out, only one dismissed? The reference must be rather to the beginning of the parable, to the calling of the Jewish people to the Faith. God called the whole people of Israel—*multi vocati*. But few among them responded—the apostles, the disciples, the first Christians—*pauci vero electi*. Jesus' words need not, then, disturb the peace of mind of the sincerely practicing member of Christ's Church.

Finally, there are the words of St. Paul: "Work out your salvation with fear and trembling" (Phil. 2:12). When I consider my own misery, I certainly have very good reason to be in fear and trembling. But looking to the divine goodness and mercy, I have immensely greater reason for confidence. The divine goodness surpasses my human misery infinitely—and exactly to that extent ought my confidence and security to exceed my fear and trembling. The fact is that this truth, "I love God," has not only a purely moral certainty. It participates after a manner in the certainty of hope, and consequently also in the certainty of faith. In order to explain this point, difficult and mysterious, let us recall that there are different classes of certitude.

In the natural order, there is scientific certitude, caused by evidence, such as two plus two equals four, and there is the certitude that rests on human authority, on the testimony of persons who are not deceived and who do not deceive us. In the supernatural order, there is the certitude of faith, which depends upon the authority of God. This is the certitude I have for divinely revealed truths. There is also the certitude of the gift of wisdom, which results from a certain connaturality or sympathy of the soul with divine things, due to the special inspiration of the Holy Spirit.

The theological virtue, hope, which relates to the possession of God in Heaven, is certain. It has not the certitude produced by evidence or by a private revelation; but as St. Thomas teaches (*ST* II-II, q. 18, art. 4), it is certain with a certitude that it derives from faith. Through hope, I have the certainty of being on the sure road that will lead to Heaven and the possession of God, guided by the infallible light of faith and relying upon the absolute trustworthiness of the promises of God. I am, moreover, in a certain way sure of arriving at the goal, because even though through my own misery I can lose my way, at least the help of God cannot fail me. I am somewhat like a person traveling by train from Chicago to New York; he is certain that he goes by a safe route and has the assurance, barring a possible but not probable accident, of arriving at his destination. Now, what is the road of salvation but grace and the virtues, especially charity or the love of God? "I love God" is then a truth that participates, after a manner, in the certainty of hope.

Once again, each of us must thrust aside false rigorism, the disagreeable aftertaste of Jansenism, and with the assurance given by Christian hope say to our Savior, "Jesus, thou knowest all things, thou seest into the very depths of my heart and thou knowest that I love thee" (see John 21:17).

God Loves Me

With more certainty still, it can be shown that God loves me. St. Paul said, "*Dilexit me*—He loved me" (Gal. 2:20). Now, he did not say these words speaking as St. Paul—that is, taking himself precisely as a saint. How far was the great apostle from believing himself a saint! He referred to himself simply as a human being, or at most a Christian. Consequently, each can appropriate St. Paul's words to himself and make them his own with full right and truth. I should not say, then, simply, in the abstract, "God loves men, God loves the human race." In a concrete, individual, and absolutely particular way, I ought to say, "God loves me." God loves me personally, just as I am. He knows me and calls me by my own proper name. "He calls his own sheep by name" (John 10:3).

To understand better the meaning of the formula "God loves me," I can meditate on the two extremes that it unites: "God and I ... God and my soul." God, the omnipotent, who has made all things from nothing; the infinite, whose perfection has no limit whatsoever; the eternal, who has neither beginning nor end and whose years, as Scripture says, "shall not fail" (Heb. 1:12); goodness itself, who has placed in all creation a trace of the tenderness of His heart; God, holiness by essence, in the presence of whom the very angels veil their faces and feel themselves stained.

And I, poor creature, less than a drop of water compared with the ocean, a grain of sand lost in the immensity of the desert, a bit of dust hanging in infinite space. I, a sinner, stained by so many falls, who have descended into that abyss more bottomless than nothing, the abyss of sin—sin committed not once but many times, so many times that I cannot count them. This God, so great, loves me who am so small; this God so good and kind, loves me who am so ungrateful; this God so holy loves me, so great a sinner.

If I could penetrate deeply into this truth, if in the fervor of prayer I could but understand it, if at the feet of my eucharistic Savior, I could by God's gift of understanding penetrate His secrets! In these three words, "God loves me," there is enough to fill my heart with joy and to fill it for eternity. They are the cause for a jubilation so intense as to place me beside myself with joy and throw me into an ecstasy of love and gratitude. But I do not comprehend these words. If I did, could I go about seeking those trifling earthly attractions that are worthless in comparison with God? Would I not rather seek only the love of God? In this love my every desire would find rest, my every anxiety peace, my every ambition satiety, my every sorrow joy. Like the saints, I would find myself intensely consoled even in the very worst hardships of life.

I should note that there is not question here of a desire: "Would that God loved me!" Nor a promise, as if God had said: "If you are good, I will love you." Neither is there question of probability: "I hope that God loves me." Nor do I believe this because some human being with authority—a priest, a prelate, a saint—has assured me of it. No, this truth, "God loves me," is a truth of faith. With an absolute certainty about it, it rests upon the authority of God and is expressly contained in Sacred Scriptures. Even in the Old Testament, God affirmed this truth many times. In the book of Proverbs, there is a plea that on the lips of God appears inconceivable: "My son, give me thy heart" (Prov. 23:26). To give one's heart is to love. God would not ask me for my love if He had not first loved me. God's plea means that He wishes His love to be requited.

To tell me more eloquently of His love, God compares it with the greatest earthly love there is: "As one whom the mother caresseth," He says, "so will I comfort you" (Isa. 66:13). "Can a woman forget her infant, so as not to have pity on the son of her womb?

And if she should forget, yet will not I forget thee" (Isa. 49:15). The Wise Man asserts that God cannot cease to love me:

> Thou hast mercy upon all, because thou canst do all things, and overlookest the sins of men for the sake of repentance. For thou lovest all things that are, and hatest none of the things which thou hast made: for thou didst not appoint, or make any thing hating it. And how could any thing endure, if thou wouldst not; or be preserved, if not called by thee? But thou sparest all: because they are thine, O Lord, who lovest souls. (Wisd. 11:24–27)

According to the Scripture, God's reason for creating me is His love for me. Now, conservation in being is a prolongation of creation, and therefore if I continue to be, the reason is that God continues to love me. I can reason legitimately then: "I exist, therefore God loves me." Am I sure of my existence? Then I can be sure that God loves me.

But the New Testament is where the affirmations of love abound, especially on the lips of our divine Savior. In the immortal pages of the Gospel according to St. John we read: "God so loved the world that he gave his only begotten Son" (John 3:16). The treasure of a father is his son. The wealth of God is His Word. And this wealth, this treasure, He gave to the world, proving His love for it. We have already seen St. Paul asserting, "Jesus loved me," and we have seen that each can apply these words personally to himself. St. Paul adds that Christ "gave himself up for me" (Gal. 2:20). Jesus' Passion and death are the great proof of His love. The Father has loved me even to the point of giving me His Son. The Son has loved me even to the point of sacrificing His life for me. Moreover, Jesus died for all men without exception. He died, consequently, for each one of us, for me, as if no one else had existed on the earth. Jesus said, "Greater love than this no one has, that one lay down his life for his friends" (John 15:13). And He did this for His enemies!

At the Last Supper, how the tender love of Jesus overflows! He speaks the almost inconceivable words: "As the Father has loved me, I also have loved you" (John 15:9). Will I ever understand, either on earth or in Heaven, the infinite love of the Father for the Son, the Son of His eternal good pleasure? This love is not, in Scholastic terminology, an accident superadded to substance as is the love of creatures; a love consequently unstable, passing, fickle, and ephemeral. God's love is a substantial, personal love, a love that is God and that is His Holy Spirit. Can I ever understand such a love as this? Well, this is the love with which Jesus has loved me. After flinging out before the world such an assurance, He had a right to add, "Abide in my love." How touching to find God petitioning His creatures not to forget Him, beseeching His creatures to love Him faithfully and forever. Jesus concludes, "These things I have spoken to you that my joy may be in you, and that your joy may be made full" (John 15:11).

What fathomless meaning in the words "As the Father has loved me, I also have loved you." First of all, as with the whole Gospel, these words are meant not only for all in general but for me in particular. "As my Father loves me, I love you in particular, my beloved son." In God there are not two loves, one for the Divine Persons among themselves and the other for creatures. There is only one love, the Holy Spirit. The Father and the Son love each other in the Holy Spirit and through the Holy Spirit. This substantial love unifies them, as the Church so frequently affirms in praying "in the unity of the Holy Spirit." Now with this same love, God loves each soul in particular and all together. Consequently, He loves each with an infinite love that cannot admit of more or less. But in His infinite love He showers grace on each according to the vocation of each. The graces of a Maria Goretti or a Br. Benildo, who live unnoticed and hidden in the world, are not the graces of a Joan of Arc, a Vincent de Paul, a Don Bosco, who have conspicuous public missions.

Besides affirming in Sacred Scripture that He loves me, God shows His love in another and even more eloquent way—the Eucharist! In the Eucharist the whole Jesus is present: His divinity, His body and soul, His virtues, His merits, His mysteries, His sacrifice, His Passion, His death—and the host that contains the whole Jesus, is it not available to every Christian every morning? After going to Communion, each of us, the very holy and the wretched alike, can say, "Jesus loves me, and because He loves me and wishes to manifest His love to me, He has given Himself to me wholly and completely in the sacred host that I have just received."

God loves me. In spite of my miseries, I also love God. Here are two fundamental truths of my Christian life. If the two of us, God and I, love each other, if we live so united that nothing can separate us, if God possesses me and I Him, and if in Him I possess the substance of eternal blessedness, what is lacking to me in order that my joy be full and perfect?

Rule 17

We cannot afford to lose sight of the truth that contemplation is far superior to activity.

We live in an age of activity. In the past, the difficulty of transportation and communication caused the rhythm of life to be slower and more restful. But now, new methods of transportation and communication have almost annihilated distance and at the same time pushed us into feverish activity in industry, commerce, business, and science. This spirit of activity expresses itself in our religious life. Never before has there been such work in the foreign mission field. And at home there has been the birth and development of Catholic Action, the participation of the laity in the apostolate of the hierarchy. Far from receiving censure, this activity deserves unstinted praise. We should encourage it with all our energies. But because of the natural human tendency to go to extremes, we must more than ever keep in mind the balance to be preserved between action and contemplation.

First, there is the question so often agitated as to which is better, action or contemplation. It may indeed seem unnecessary to raise this question. Even the Greek philosophers, pagans though they were, affirmed that contemplation is of itself superior to action. Aristotle said that the "intellectual" life is better than the "human" life, that immanent or vital activity is superior to transient and nonvital activity. Only the modern philosopher has thought of considering immanent activity, the activity of the intelligence for example, as a mere transient and productive activity.

The Christian has even more reason to affirm the supremacy of contemplation. In a famous scene in Bethany, Jesus defended Mary, the contemplative, against the complaints of her more active sister, Martha. "Mary has chosen the best part, and it will not be taken away from her" (Luke 10:42).

St. Augustine has drawn a very beautiful comparison of the active life with the contemplative, making it clear why the latter is better, and pointing out that because it is better, it will never end: "The Church knows that there are two lives," he says,

> which God has revealed to it and has praised. One is lived in faith, the other in vision; one in the time of exile, the other in the mansion of eternity; one in work, the other in rest; one along the road of pilgrimage, the other in the home land; one in the place of struggle and work, the other in the joy of contemplation.
>
> One avoids evil and does good, the other knows no evil to avoid, but a great good to enjoy; one fights against the enemy, the other reigns without an adversary; one comes to the help of the needy, the other has no unfortunate to succor; one pardons others the offenses which it receives in order to obtain forgiveness of its own, the other receives no offenses to pardon, nor does it do anything that requires it to ask for pardon; one is scourged with afflictions in order that it may not become proud of the good it has, the other is filled with such abundance of graces that it is protected from all evil and can adhere to the supreme good without the least temptation to pride.
>
> The one, then, is good, but full of miseries, the other is better and is blessed. The one is passed completely on

earth; it will endure to the end of time and then will cease. The other, to attain its perfection, must wait until the end of the world. But in the future world it will have no end.

St. Thomas Aquinas (*ST* II–II, q. 182, art. 1), teaching that the contemplative life is better than the active, produces eight reasons drawn from philosophical considerations and reinforced with texts from Sacred Scripture. They can be summarized as follows:

1. A man exercises the contemplative life by his most perfect faculty, the intellect, which attains to spiritual reality. The active life, on the other hand, is exercised through the powers man has in common with the brute animals, and it has for its object exterior things. The Old Testament signifies this difference in Rachel and Lia. The contemplative life is represented by Rachel, whose name signifies "vision of the source," while Lia, whose eyes are weak, represents the active life.

2. The contemplative life can be more continuous. In it we can always be united to God, while the active life is necessarily intermittent. Accordingly, Mary, symbol of the contemplative life, remains seated at the feet of the Savior while her sister is going to and fro.

3. The joy produced by the contemplative life is greater than the joy produced by the active life. But that which produces greater spiritual joy is of itself better. St. Augustine notes that while Martha was troubled, Mary rejoiced.

4. Peace is more secure in the contemplative life, because in it fewer things are desired. Jesus said, "Martha, Martha, thou art anxious and troubled about many things" (Luke 10:41).

5. The contemplative life is sought for its own sake, while the active life is sought for the sake of something else. Action belongs only to the order of means, while contemplation is of the order of ends. Contemplation excels action, then, as the end excels the means. The Psalmist indicates this when he says, "One thing I have asked of the Lord, this will I seek after: that I may dwell in the house of the Lord all the days of my life. That I may see the delight of the Lord" (Ps. 26:4).

6. The contemplative life consists in a kind of rest that is of higher value than work. This rest is not idleness but the consummation of activity, for it is the repose of our faculties in the possession of God. The Psalmist expresses this characteristic of contemplation, saying, "Be still, and see that I am God" (Ps. 45:11).

7. The contemplative life is concerned with divine things, but the active life with human things. St. Augustine says, " 'In the beginning was the Word' — behold the one to whom Mary was listening — 'and the Word was made flesh' — behold the one whom Martha was serving."

8. Finally, Jesus Himself declared, "Mary has chosen the best part, and it will not be taken away from her" (Luke 10:42). St. Augustine explains our Lord's meaning like this: "It is not that the way of Martha is bad, but that the way of Mary is better. Why better? Because it will not be taken away from her. One day we shall see ourselves free from this burden which necessity imposes (the active life); but the sweetness of the contemplation of the Truth is eternal."

In explanation of the teaching of St. Thomas, we might add that the active life consists in the exercise of the moral virtues, contemplation in the exercise of the theological virtues. The moral virtues remove obstacles to man's union with God, but the theological virtues achieve the consummation of the Christian life by actually uniting us to Him. Action is of earth; contemplation is of Heaven. Action halts at the threshold of eternity, while contemplation is made perfect in Heaven, its home.

Presumably anyone will admit that in theory contemplation is better than action. But how many in practice give the first place to action! Not only the indifferent and the religiously careless do it, but the devout as well. Even those with some public dignity in the Church, whose example cannot fail to make an impression on the simple faithful, must take care here.

In order to resolve difficulties involved in the question of action and contemplation, there is nowadays much talk of a third class of life, the mixed life, in which action and contemplation are combined. But it seems that into this division of active, contemplative, and mixed lives, there sometimes creeps a certain confusion.

First, the active and contemplative lives are not exactly a *division* of the Christian *life*. They are not two lives running side by side like parallel lines, so that some Christians are to follow the way of the active life and others the way of the contemplative life. Rather—and this is of capital importance—the active and the contemplative lives are two stages along an identical road. They are two phases of one spiritual life. According to God's plan, all men ought to pass through both. Moreover, only in our mind and by abstraction are the two stages found separately. In concrete reality, instead of being completely isolated, they more or less interpenetrate. This means that the spiritual life is not an exclusively active life. It means also that there cannot be a truly contemplative life that is not fruitful and does not redound to the good of others. Now, if in concrete reality neither action nor contemplation can exist in isolation, then the spiritual life must be always a combination of action and contemplation. Action will predominate in the beginner, contemplation in the advanced.

What, in fact, is the mixed life as a special way of Christian living? It can have meaning not as applied to the intimate nature of the spiritual life, but only to its exterior manifestations, to someone's daily program and occupation. Religious orders and congregations are called "active," "contemplative," or "mixed" by reason of the employment to which they are dedicated—and not because religious in the first group lead a purely active life, those in the second a purely contemplative life, and those in the third combine the two.

Every Christian ought to combine the two lives. However great his exterior activity, he ought to be a contemplative within. The more he has to occupy himself with his neighbor, the more he needs union with God. "Without contemplation," says Fr. Lallemant,

> we shall never progress sufficiently in virtue nor shall we be capable of helping others advance. We shall never free ourselves completely from our weaknesses and imperfections. We shall remain attached to the earth and shall never succeed in elevating ourselves sufficiently above the sentiments of our human nature. We shall be unable to render to God a perfect service. But with contemplation we shall do more for ourselves and for others in a month than we could do without it in ten years.

St. John of the Cross asks, "Of what use are those who prefer activity and imagine that they are going to conquer the world with their preaching and their external works?" He continues, "What are they doing? Something more than nothing; sometimes absolutely nothing; sometimes, instead of doing good, they do harm."

Contemplation, itself the supreme activity, makes all other activities fruitful. Contemplatives do the most good in the Church of God, because by their prayer and sacrifice they obtain the grace that moves hearts and converts wills. True apostles, missionaries who have the spirit of God, attach more importance to the army of those who pray than to the army of those who fight, to hands raised to Heaven to beg divine grace than to those lowered to earth to remedy its miseries, to the lips that speak to God about men than to the lips that speak to men about God. This is why upon arriving in a mission country, their first concern is to establish a monastery of contemplatives to be a "leaven that leavens the whole mass." They see the need for a focal point of the interior life, to draw down blessings from Heaven. When His Holiness Pope Pius XI assigned as patrons of Catholic missions St. Francis Xavier and St. Thérèse of the Child Jesus, one an apostle and the other a contemplative, did he not proclaim to the world this great truth of the indissoluble union of action and contemplation and the mutual influence of each on the other?

The spiritual life has in reality three stages: active, contemplative, and apostolic. In the active or ascetical life, obstacles to union with God are taken away. The moral virtues are exercised and a person is placed in proper order with reference to his neighbor and himself. In the contemplative or mystical life, we are united to God through the exercise of the theological virtues and the predominating activity of the gifts of the Holy Spirit. Finally, the apostolic life is the fruit of the contemplative life, its overflow on behalf of one's neighbor. If a man is perfectly united to God, he will inevitably be powerfully moved by zeal for his neighbor's welfare. A priest will faithfully carry out his duties to teach and administer the sacraments. A member of the simple faithful will pray, sacrifice, and carry out the apostolate proper to his station.

St. Thomas Aquinas understands by the mixed life not the combination of the active and contemplative lives but the apostolic life. In the apostolic life, the contemplative communicates to others the fruits of his contemplation. "*Contemplari et contemplata aliis tradere*—to contemplate and to hand on to others what has been contemplated" (*ST* II-II, q. 188, art. 6). Rather than being a combination of the active and contemplative lives, the mixed life is in this way seen as the fullness and consummation of the contemplative life. The mixed or apostolic life can, then, hardly be described as superior to the contemplative life, any more than the fruit can be called superior to the tree that produces it. The apostolic life is but the contemplative life communicated, just as the charity that causes us to love and serve God and our neighbor is one charity.

The contemplative life is related to the apostolic life as the Incarnation is related to the Redemption. The first is the eminent cause, the second the marvelous fruit. The Incarnation, the hypostatic union of the divine and human natures, is not inferior to nor subordinated to the Redemption, although it is intimately related to it as the tree to its fruit. Neither is the contemplative life subordinated to the apostolic life or inferior to it. The contemplative life produces the apostolic life as its effect and fruit. To deny this would be to fall into the absurdity of affirming that the service of God (contemplative life) is subordinated to and inferior to the service of one's neighbor (apostolic life). The Christian apostolate, then, is not and cannot be anything but the overflow of contemplation, the crumbs that fall to the earth from the banquet in which God and the soul give themselves to each other in ineffable communion. The reason why superficial minds do not understand the contemplative life in relation to the apostolic life is that the apostolate can be seen while contemplation remains hidden. Setting more store by what appears than by what does not, attaching more importance to what makes a noise than to what is silent within, these minds cannot understand that the apostolate has its source in the inner quiet of contemplation.

We can conclude, first of all, that in our spiritual growth the active life is the preparation, the means, the road for arriving at the contemplative life.

Second, in practice the one life cannot be disassociated from the other. The reason the active life cannot be separated from the contemplative is that the moral virtues cannot be exercised without the theological virtues of faith, hope, and charity. The exercise of the theological virtues in turn cannot fail to produce in the soul a contemplation of the mysteries of God, at least incipiently, and if contemplation be taken broadly. The reason why the contemplative life cannot prescind from the active life is that in contemplation there must continue to exist at least the fruit obtained through the practice of the moral virtues. Moreover, under the influence of the gifts, the soul enters into a great activity, exercising the moral virtues in a perfect manner. Under the influence of the gifts, the soul is more humble, meek, patient, strong, moderate, just, and prudent than ever.

Third, we must note that while, strictly speaking, the contemplative life can take on various forms—hence the magnificent variety to be admired among God's saints—this life expresses itself in two ways in particular, one more purely contemplative, the other oriented toward activity. The contemplative or mystical life consists in the predominance of the gifts of the Holy Spirit. These gifts can be divided into two great groups: the contemplative gifts (knowledge, understanding, and wisdom) and the active gifts (fear of the Lord, piety, counsel, and fortitude). When the active gifts develop in a special way and the contemplative gifts themselves have a certain orientation toward activity, there is produced the mystic apostle. St. Vincent de Paul, the Curé of Ars, and St. John Bosco are examples. When the contemplative gifts develop in a special way and remain specifically contemplative, then there result the mystical contemplatives, such as St. Francis of Assisi, St. John of the Cross, St. Teresa of Jesus, and St. Thérèse of Lisieux. In these latter, contemplation is typical and manifest; in the others, it is nontypical and veiled. But both types of saints are contemplative, for contemplation is the "soul of the apostolate" and the prelude to the blessed life in Heaven.

Rule 18

The transforming union is the summit of the spiritual life and the prelude to beatitude.

How much good it does us to breathe the fresh air of the mountains! There where the surroundings are purer, the atmosphere clearer, solitude friendlier, and the heavens nearer! A mere glimpse of supernatural summits has a similarly invigorating effect. We may be far from the height of sanctity ourselves, plodding along and hardly seeming to be making any progress up the steep incline of the purgative and illuminative ways. Yet in contemplating the heights that we aspire to reach, we renew our strength, revive our enthusiasm, and inflame our hope.

The summit of the spiritual life is the transforming union. True antechamber to Heaven and a point all Christians ought normally to reach, it is in fact attained by few. Admittedly, the transforming union is a mystical state; and as no one can attain mystical gifts by his own powers, even aided by grace, certainly the greatest of all these gifts, the transforming union, is not to be so attained. Yet when a person generously complies with all that God asks of him, God, who calls all to holiness, will not deny mystical graces or frustrate lawful aspirations.

It is a comforting teaching, commonly admitted and taught today, that mysticism is not something extraordinary and miraculous, like the gift of miracles or prophecy. Mysticism is not to be confused with certain secondary and accidental phenomena that sometimes accompany it, such as levitation, ecstasy, stigmatization, or the gift of scrutiny of hearts. Genuine mysticism is simply the full and normal development of sanctifying grace, the infused virtues, and the gifts of the Holy Spirit. In the spiritual life, there are not two parallel roads, one ascetical and the other mystical; there is only one way. Like all divine works, the spiritual life has perfect unity. Asceticism and mysticism are but two stages of one journey, two periods in one ascent toward God. In the ascetical stage, an individual is exercised in the virtues, while in the mystical, the gifts predominate. In the ascetical life, the individual operates actively, practicing the virtues in a way that is human although supernaturalized by grace. In the mystical life, he is said to act passively, the Holy Spirit moving him in His activity through the mediation of the gifts. Under the motion of the Holy Spirit, a person really enters into a new and more intense activity, as he exercises the virtues under the influence of the gifts and consequently in a superhuman or divine way.

If holiness is simply our *divinization* or our becoming godlike, the transforming union is our perfect *divinization*. What path do those follow who arrive at this summit? First, we must understand that there is a distinction in man between being and activity. Nature cannot act directly through itself in man or in any other creature; it needs faculties, and these in turn must be put into operation. The act of understanding, for example, requires not only a spiritual nature but a spiritual nature perfected by a special faculty, the intellect. The intellect, in turn, must be put into activity if understanding is actually to take place.

There is a parallel in the supernatural order. Meritorious supernatural acts require that the soul be supernaturalized by sanctifying grace. But beyond this, the faculties of intellect and will must also be supernaturalized by the infused virtues and gifts. Finally, the virtues and gifts have to be put into exercise by means of actual graces. In other words, our divinization has two aspects: both our nature and our activity must be made godlike. Sanctifying grace does the first; the virtues, gifts, and actual graces do the second.

When we receive Baptism worthily and as long as we are in the state of grace, our nature and our faculties are radically supernaturalized by our possession of sanctifying grace with its inseparable retinue of virtues and gifts. God denies His actual graces to no one in the state of grace, and with the aid of these actual graces, we begin to exercise the virtues and to do good works. The moral virtues, proper to the active life, take away the obstacles that stand between ourselves and God, while the theological virtues, exercised especially in prayer, begin to unite us to God. Exercising the virtues or performing the good acts that proceed from the virtues, we begin to acquire merit and our spiritual wealth becomes daily greater. Now, the immediate result of merit is to increase sanctifying grace and to make the soul grow in virtue—grace and the virtues both increasing together. Meanwhile, the individual is purified by his exercise of the various virtues, including all the exercises of the active life, especially mortification and penance. This is active purification.

As a result of active purification, an individual arrives at the threshold of the illuminative way. God intervenes to begin a new purification. When the moment arrives in which the soul cannot actively purify itself further, the Holy Spirit steps in to carry on the purification by means of the gifts of fear, fortitude, and knowledge.

This is called the passive purification or, in the terminology of St. John of the Cross, the dark night of the senses. It may be likened to a surgical operation in which the patient remains passive, while the surgeon cuts into the infected part of the body. In the dark night of the senses, God anesthetizes the sensibility of the soul by means of aridity, while at the same time His purifying fire destroys all its disorders. Having been purified in this way, one comes to a new knowledge of God (infused prayer) and begins to love God with a love not present before (infused love).

But a new and more intimate purification is still needed, the night of the Spirit. In this night the Holy Spirit employs the gift of understanding to purify the higher faculties of the soul—the intellect and the will. As a result, the individual can enter fully into infused contemplation and the love of God, where the gift of wisdom has a special role to play. It should be noted, nevertheless, that the mystical life does not always have a marked contemplative flavor. According to the designs of God for each individual, some gift other than wisdom can predominate. There are those who are conspicuous for their spirit of compunction, for example, in whom the gift of fear predominates. Others have a capacity for governing and a special mission to direct souls; in these, the gift of counsel has a directive role. In those outstanding for their apostolic labor, the gift of piety is dominant.

When someone reaches the loftiest spiritual heights after years of exercising the virtues not only in a human way but also under the influence of the gifts, the merits he has stored up are incalculable, and incalculable also the fullness of sanctifying grace that divinizes him. Since the gifts of the Holy Spirit now predominate in his activity, he almost never does anything except as directed by the Holy

Spirit. Insofar as it is to be achieved in this life, he has attained the perfect divinization of the Christian, in both being and activity. To one so supernaturalized, God unites Himself so intimately that there can be no greater union for him except in Heaven. Such is the transforming union considered in its substance.

Though the transforming union is always essentially the same, it may in practice manifest a striking variety. There are three principal variations. When the dominant note is love, the transforming union is called spiritual marriage. When it is sacrifice or immolation, the transforming union can be called eucharistic transformation. When the outstanding characteristic is spiritual fecundity, the union can be called mystical incarnation.

St. John of the Cross and St. Teresa speak only of the first variety of the transforming union, spiritual marriage. The second is especially characteristic of the religious life of our times, when devotion to the Blessed Sacrament has achieved such a remarkable development. In this expression of the transforming union, the soul becomes truly a victim or "host," assimilated to the Holy Eucharist in the most perfect possible way. The crowning fruit of eucharistic piety, this union is the result of many fervent sacramental Communions, which gradually transform the soul into a living Eucharist.

With respect to the third type of the transforming union, its name need not surprise us if its meaning be understood correctly. The Incarnation of the Word is uniquely and exclusively with the humanity of Jesus Christ. But in God's plan the humanity of Christ is the means by which each one of us is to be united to God. The hypostatic union is with the humanity of Christ alone. But there is another kind of union between Christ and the soul by grace. Sr.

Elizabeth of the Trinity[5] very rightly wanted to be a prolongation of the humanity of Christ. All Christians in grace are in fact this, though more especially those who are perfect and holy.

Just as the Word made hypostatically His own the humanity of Jesus Christ (who is the Word), so, due proportion being kept, He makes others His own in another way. And for what purpose? For the same purpose that motivated the Incarnation: to redeem the world, and so to glorify the Father. Is there, then, anything strange in the notion that when one arrives at the height of the transforming union, the union may take on this special aspect of being a prolongation of the humanity of Christ, in order to continue in the world His fruitful work? And why should we not be able to give to the transforming union considered under this special aspect the name of "mystical incarnation"?

Certainly, the individual continues to maintain his own proper personality. But the union with the Word is so intimate that the Word takes this blessed soul as a prolongation of His own proper humanity, in order to continue in it, insofar as possible, the mysteries of His mortal life, the Incarnation, the Nativity, the hidden life, the public life, the Passion, and death.

Msgr. Gay says very beautifully that "it is necessary to be Jesus if one is to do the work of Jesus." One who has been transformed into Jesus, and who therefore is mystically Jesus, has the task of continuing the work of Jesus. In the soul in which He mystically reproduces the mysteries of His mortal life, Jesus continues His work of glorifying the Father and redeeming the world. It does not appear to us too bold to suppose that the transforming union in this special aspect was first realized in the Blessed Virgin — in her before any other and as in no other. For besides being the

---

[5] St. Elizabeth of the Trinity was canonized October 2016. — Ed.

natural Mother of Christ, she is also His Mother in a mystical way. She is the co-redemptrix of the world, the mediatrix of all grace, and the Mother of all men. What is proper to this mode of the transforming union is that it gives to the soul a mysterious and delicate character of fecundity and maternity. The soul possesses a mystical maternity with reference to others and also, in a certain sense, with reference to Jesus. Any relation with the Mystical Body of Jesus always arises from a relation with the head, which is Jesus.

The love, then, with which one loves Jesus is a love that might be called maternal, insofar as it is possible to name with human words the lofty and hidden realities of mysticism. In the words of Archbishop Martinez:

> The mission of a soul which has received the grace of spiritual fecundity is to conceive and give birth to Jesus mystically, spreading Him around about it like a gently radiating light, like a perfume which makes everything around it fragrant. Such a soul is to Jesus a mother; in unspeakable mystery, it has for Him a new name, a new love, a new and most sweet mission. In this holy and supreme fecundity are concentrated and merged all the spiritual prerogatives of the soul: its lights, its purity, its love, its sacrifice. All these divine things have as their center and crown this virginal fecundity the fruit of which is Jesus.
>
> For this reason the supreme rest for these souls is in fruitfulness. As the ancient Patriarchs rested in their desires and in their hopes when they received from the Lord the promise that their descendants would be multiplied as the stars of the sky; as the Blessed Virgin rested in a heavenly way when she pressed against her heart her most sweet Son and when she saw in Him, more numerous than the stars

of heaven, the innumerable souls redeemed through His blood and incorporated into Him through faith and love; so souls which have received from God the singular gift of spiritual maternity, find their rest in pressing to their heart the divine Jesus and in Him all the souls, to whom, according to the divine designs, His vital influence is to extend. What a magnificent mission! What a sublime rest!

The Gospel tells us how on one occasion our Lord's Blessed Mother and some of His relations wished to speak with Him. They could not get near to Him because of the multitude surrounding Him. When someone said to Him, "Your mother and your brothers desire to speak with You," He answered, "Who is a mother and who are brothers to me?" Then extending His arms toward His disciples, He said, "Here are my mother and my brothers. Everyone who does the will of my Father who is in Heaven, he is my brother and sister and mother" (see Matt. 12:46–50). Commenting on these words, St. Gregory says that it is not remarkable that those who carry out the will of the Father should be called brothers and sisters of the Lord. But that they could also be called "mother of Christ" does appear surprising. St. Gregory explains it through the mystery of the priesthood, especially through the ministry of preaching, which causes Christ to be born in souls, giving birth to Him in them.

St. Paul does not fear to say, "My dear children, with whom I am in labor again, until Christ is formed in you" (Gal. 4:19). Now, this privilege of forming Christ in souls belongs in a special manner to the hierarchical priesthood. But it belongs also to the mystical priesthood of the faithful in another way. This mystical priesthood is realized in none so perfectly as in souls who have been transformed into Christ with this special character of fecundity that we have called mystical incarnation. To be sure, very little, almost nothing, has been written about this, the ultimate stage of the spiritual life. Fr. Poulain, S.J., author of the well-known treatise on mysticism *The Graces of Interior Prayer*, was consulted on this matter a short time before his death and answered, "Alas, nothing has been written on this fourth stage of the spiritual life."

Perhaps so little has been said on this subject because of the fear that souls might beguile themselves into following the lamentable path of false mysticism, a path that can have such frightful consequences for souls and for the Church. Possibly the reason for this silence is that it is not prudent to speak of something that one does not know through personal experience. Whatever the case may be, may we be pardoned in our littleness for having tried to treat in hesitant words of such lofty, divine mysteries.

Conclusion

Frequently one finds among Catholics the notion that the spiritual life is purely negative, simply a matter of avoiding sin. When grace touches the soul of the careless Christian and he turns seriously to God, he is likely to concentrate all his efforts on maintaining himself in the state of grace and avoiding mortal sin. Venial sin may seem of little consequence to him. If he tries to rise higher, he will concentrate his efforts on avoiding deliberate venial sin and on rooting out defects one by one. He may further set his sights on growth in the moral virtues, such as humility, mortification, patience. Since these virtues are concerned with removing obstacles to union with God, they pertain rather to the negative than to the positive aspect of Christian life. When an individual has more or less succeeded in carrying out this negative program, he may look around wondering what to do next. The horizons close down around him, and his spiritual life comes to a standstill.

Yet the horizons of the spiritual life are truly limitless, pointing as they do to the infinite God. God gives souls wings to fly, to lose themselves in the divine immensity. But through the want of understanding on the part of these individuals, their wings are tied. What would we say of a man who conceived of human life as only the absence of sickness—who reduced his life to the careful prevention of illness by strict observance of the rules of hygiene, and to the cure of sickness when, in spite of his precautions, it came upon him? We should certainly say that his notion of life was negative and impoverished! A man's life cannot consist in merely continuing to exist and in avoiding sickness. Life is positive; it demands that we enter into integral human activity and exercise all our faculties. Truly human life consists especially in the activity of our spiritual powers of intellect and will. We want to know the truth and to love what it is good for us to love.

Now, if natural life must point to something positive, supernatural life must no less do so. It does not consist merely in avoiding sin. It does not lie principally even in the exercise of the moral virtues; as these have as their objects the removal of obstacles, they, too, in one respect are negative. The spiritual life consists positively in the full activity of those great supernatural gifts that put us in touch with God. Faith causes us to know God; hope makes us look for Him with keen desire; charity unites us with Him in a most intimate embrace that is, considered purely in itself, definitive. A person who lives the Christian life is one who believes, and hopes, and loves.

We can understand better the positive character of the Christian life if we recall that it is essentially a family and a social life. In the natural order, family life consists in the association between parents and children. Parents must provide the material necessities for their children and educate them by giving them due instruction, counsel, and correction. Children must obey, respect, and honor their parents and mutually help one another materially and morally. The family association is based on the love that binds together and unites the members of the family. Love is the indispensable foundation and the sacred unity of the home.

Conclusion

Social life is made up of our associations with friends and acquaintances, and others with whom we come in contact. In these associations, we must respect the rights of others, fulfilling our contracted obligations, rendering mutual services and favors. In friendship there is, besides, the special love that unites friends in the fulfilling of the mutual offices that love implies. Social life is based, if not always on love properly so called, at least on mutual esteem and respect.

Now, the spiritual life is a family and social life transplanted to the supernatural order. God is truly our Father, more truly and by a title incomparably superior to that of the parent who played a part in bringing us into the world. It is a distinctive boldness of Christianity to direct mankind to address God by the most familiar name of Father. Through Christ, men are in reality God's sons. Our supernatural sonship is a genuine reality, if a hidden one. St. John says, "Behold what manner of love the Father has bestowed upon us, that we should be called children of God; and such we are.... Beloved, now we are the children of God, and it has not yet appeared what we shall be" (1 John 3:1-2).

The incarnate Word is our Brother. A man like us, He belongs to the same race of Adam, the same great human family. In a more special way, He is our Brother because we are sons of His Father through the sanctifying grace that we gain through Him. This grace is distinctively filial because it comes from Him, the Son. Sanctifying grace incorporates us into Christ, makes us sons with the Son, so that His Father is now ours. It is in this sense that St. Paul calls Jesus "the firstborn among many brethren" (Rom. 8:29).

As sons of the Father and brothers of Jesus Christ, we receive life from their Spirit, the Holy Spirit, who makes us cry, "Abba, Father" (Gal. 4:6). This Spirit gives testimony to our spirit that we are the sons of God. We enter into the company of the three

Divine Persons themselves, as St. John says (see John 1:3). We are no longer strangers, outsiders, or even simple guests. We are of the family of God and fellow citizens of the saints (cf. Eph. 2:19).

The most Blessed Virgin, the Mother of God, is our Mother also. For she became the Mother of Christ according to nature in order to be the Mother of all men according to grace. She is the Mother of the whole Christ, the Mystical Body, which contains in wonderful unity Jesus the head and His loyal followers as members. The Gospel says that Mary gave birth to her "firstborn." Due to have no other children according to nature, she would bring forth a multitude according to grace so as to be the Mother of all.

Besides Christ's Mother, all the angels and blessed in Heaven are our constant companions. An angel has been appointed by God to assist, protect, and guide us here on earth. The saint whose name we bear is on the lookout in a special way to help us. All the angels and saints are actively interested in our salvation and sanctification; they especially intercede for us when we call upon them. When we neglect them, the Church calls upon them for us, as on the feast of All Saints and in her litanies.

Our Christian life is indeed a family life with God, the Father, Son, and Holy Spirit. It is a social life with the angels and saints. But as these realities cannot be perceived with our senses and cannot be comprehended by natural reason alone, the supernatural virtues of faith, hope, and charity are indispensable. Faith discovers these divine realities. Hope makes us desire them. And charity permits us to communicate with them.

In our Christian life we are not limited, however, to association with the Church Triumphant. The Church Triumphant, the Church Suffering, and the Church Militant are so united that they are not so much three churches as three successive stages of the one Church of Jesus Christ. Consequently, the Christian life includes our association with all other men on the supernatural level. The same virtue of faith that manifests supernatural realities transforms our fellow man before our eyes. Instead of seeing merely human failings, we discover the divine image in our fellow man and we understand the grandeur of sanctifying grace. We see about us images of God, members of the Body of Christ, future citizens in the City of God and the heavenly Jerusalem. Moreover, what faith manifests on earth it manifests more tellingly in the souls in Purgatory, now confirmed in grace. This knowledge that faith gives us blossoms forth in charity toward all. We understand that each can raise his eyes to Heaven and say, "Our Father ..." Here is the universal Christian charity that has inspired such heroism through the centuries.

What is true of the Christian life in general is true also of the religious life, which is its most perfect expression. One can fall into the same error of conceiving it also under a negative aspect only. The religious life will then be conceived as consisting only in the avoiding of sins, but the religious must take into account not only the prohibitions that bind all but also the innumerable special ones that bind him. The religious has to avoid everything that is prohibited by the law of God and the precepts of the Church. In addition, he must avoid everything prohibited by the vows of poverty, chastity, and obedience; everything that the law of the cloister forbids; everything prohibited by the rule, constitutions, ordinances, and precepts of superiors. "There remains very little that a religious can do!" one is tempted to exclaim. A nun cannot go out of her convent, because the law of enclosure forbids it. She cannot on her own decision dispose of a single red cent, because the vow of poverty will not allow it. She cannot set up a home and enjoy its legitimate satisfactions, because the vow of chastity forbids it. She cannot make an act of her own will, because she is bound by the vow of obedience. From the moment that she answers the first bell in the morning until she retires at night, constitutions, rules, and house regulations indicate for her what she is to do. In fact, twenty-four hours a day, her time is not her own.

If this were the whole story of the religious life, an interminable chain of prohibitions, it would be inhuman and unbearable. Fortunately, this is only half the story. All the negations are but the efficacious means for the removal of obstacles. One must detach oneself from creature and self, but only in order to take full wing and fly into the arms of God. The positive aspect of the religious life is companionship with God, a companionship all the more familiar as one is more emptied and detached. The religious ought, as no other, to live a life of faith, hope, and love. In the religious above all is to be realized the "stupendous familiarity" with God of which the *Imitation* speaks. The hope of a religious should be a more vital hope, for it rests not only on our Lord's general promises but also on a very particular one: "Everyone who has left house, or brothers, or sisters, or father, or mother, or wife, or children, or lands, for my name's sake, shall receive a hundredfold, and shall possess life everlasting" (Matt. 19:29). The charity of a religious ought to be more ardent, nourished by the fire of sacrifice that the religious life itself is.

We spoke earlier of the importance of balance in the spiritual life. Nowhere is balance more urgent than in this matter of the positive and the negative. There is the perpetual temptation to consider only the negative or only the positive, while in fact the two aspects must be combined. It would be a vain illusion to try to unite ourselves to God without purifying ourselves of sin, just as to think only of avoiding sin would be to leave our spiritual

Conclusion

life truncated and mutilated. But if the two elements are inseparable and both are necessary, the positive is definitely the more important. The negative removes the obstacles; the Christian life consists especially in the positive.

We must purify ourselves from sin, always aiming at the positive goal of union with God. We will indeed try to live in a state of grace. We will work to avoid deliberate venial sin and even, insofar as is possible to our human frailty, semideliberate venial sins. We will work to correct our defects. We will practice the moral virtues. But before all and above all, let us not lose sight of the fact that the true Christian life consists specifically in conversation and union with God. Fr. Félix Rougier, the holy founder of the Missionaries of the Holy Ghost, was accustomed toward the end of his life to say one word over and over; in his letters and conversations he would repeat with the fervor of a saint, "God ... God ... God ..." And with what good reason! Does not this one word sum up all the spiritual experience that one can have? Toward the end of their lives, very holy individuals frequently find that there is nothing more to say. They have so well understood the vanity of everything created that there remains for them but this one supreme reality. It is as when the sun comes up—then all the stars are hidden and all other lights turn pale. Purely human life is the night, life with God the day. Blessed is the soul from whose heaven the shadows of night have fled and for whom there shines only the brightness of God!

St. Francis of Assisi expressed this truth when he exclaimed, "*Deus meus et omnia*—my God and my All!" And St. Teresa of Jesus in saying, "To him who has God, nothing is lacking. God alone suffices." And St. Paul summed up the whole of God's plan, the entire purpose of the Redemption, when he said, "*Ut Deus sit omnia in omnibus*—that God may be all in all" (1 Cor. 15:28).

Rules for the Spiritual Life

A holy woman of our own time, the French mystic Lucie Christine, has written a sublime page describing her own experience of this "allness" of God:

> My soul understood that it must live in the most Blessed Trinity, with that life from on high, far above everything else. It understood that while it must lend itself to every duty, it must surrender itself to God alone....
>
> Afterwards, as if heaven had half opened a little, I heard the universal concert of the angels and of the elect honoring the most Blessed Trinity. I perceived in the future as in a point, in a glance quicker than a lightning flash, all the voices of the world dying and coming to an end in the canticle of immortality,... the voice of genius, the voice of knowledge, the voice of strength and power, the voice of love and tenderness of heart, the voice of valor, the voice of the imagination, the voice of hope and fear, the voice of joy and sorrow, the voice of all activities and tumults, the voice of nature and of tempests and of thunder, the voice of the events and cataclysms that change the face of empires, and vibrate in the depths of the world and shake the balance of the human race from the top to its foundation. All this will become extinct, all this will be silent. In one day all this will give place to the eternal *alleluia* to which my soul now listens....
>
> Apart from the unfortunates condemned to eternal hate and to God's punishments, there will be but one cry, one only: "*Sanctus, Sanctus, Sanctus*; Holy, Holy, Holy," to the glory of that God who is thrice holy, the Father, Son, and Holy Spirit....
>
> O sublime region, region of love, only region in which the soul can find a new day, a new life, an air to breathe,...

where only God appears and all else remains in shadow, ... where the soul, lost in Jesus only, adores and can do nothing but adore, or rather where Jesus adores in it! ... Divine rest in the omnipotence which has lowered itself to our soul through love; repose unknown to the world, repose in the Truth itself; thirst of the soul, rapturously satiated by the infinite; supreme confusion of a sinful nothing before its God, which, however, does not take note even of this in order to humiliate itself more profoundly, for it does not and cannot see anything but its Creator!

Oh, Father, Teacher, Friend, Spouse...! Why must I again descend from that region where You are, O my Beloved? We are so happy together in solitude...! You speak to me and I to You without a word.... You find Your delight in my soul taking all that Your love has put there; and I, no longer seeing anything on earth, feel myself lost in You.... Why must I descend from that heavenly region which is You, my God?

About the Author

Very Rev. Don José de Guadalupe Treviño was a native of Mexico. He was ordained to the priesthood in 1914 and taught at the Grand Seminary of Morelia, Michoacan, where he became prefect. He received the religious habit in the Congregation of Missionaries of the Holy Ghost in 1918. In 1944, he was elected vicar-general. He authored several books, including *The Holy Eucharist*.

Sophia Institute

Sophia Institute is a nonprofit institution that seeks to nurture the spiritual, moral, and cultural life of souls and to spread the gospel of Christ in conformity with the authentic teachings of the Roman Catholic Church.

Sophia Institute Press fulfills this mission by offering translations, reprints, and new publications that afford readers a rich source of the enduring wisdom of mankind.

Sophia Institute also operates the popular online resource CatholicExchange.com. *Catholic Exchange* provides world news from a Catholic perspective as well as daily devotionals and articles that will help readers to grow in holiness and live a life consistent with the teachings of the Church.

In 2013, Sophia Institute launched Sophia Institute for Teachers to renew and rebuild Catholic culture through service to Catholic education. With the goal of nurturing the spiritual, moral, and cultural life of souls, and an abiding respect for the role and work of teachers, we strive to provide materials and programs that are at once enlightening to the mind and ennobling to the heart; faithful and complete, as well as useful and practical.

Sophia Institute gratefully recognizes the Solidarity Association for preserving and encouraging the growth of our apostolate over the course of many years. Without their generous and timely support, this book would not be in your hands.

www.SophiaInstitute.com
www.CatholicExchange.com
www.SophiaInstituteforTeachers.org

Sophia Institute Press is a registered trademark of Sophia Institute.
Sophia Institute is a tax-exempt institution as defined by the
Internal Revenue Code, Section 501(c)(3). Tax ID 22-2548708.